Hamly

I. O.

The Earth

illustrated by John Smith

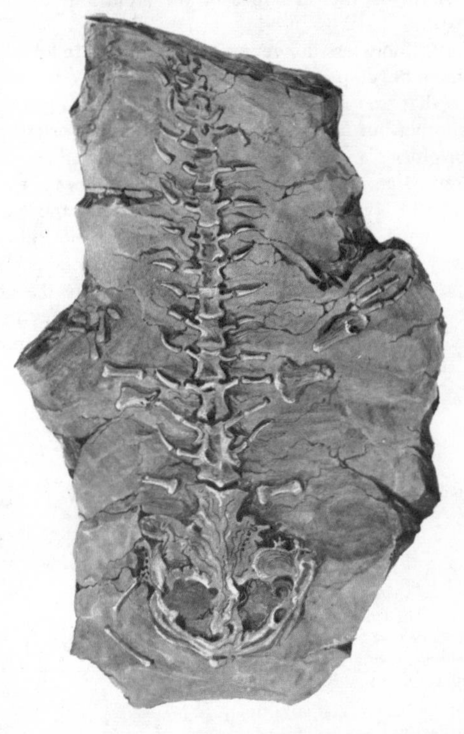

Hamlyn - London
Sun Books - Melbourne

FOREWORD

Now that the printed word has been reinforced by radio and television, most of us have a general idea of the findings of modern science regarding the world on which we live. We think of the Earth as a small planet in an immense Universe, millions of years old and inhabited by creatures that, including ourselves, have evolved slowly from very simple forms of life, or possibly even from non-living matter. We may even have a vague inkling of some of the recent views on the structure of the atom and the nature of the Universe.

We may know less, however, about the way in which our modern views have developed since the days in which our forefathers, who believed that they lived on a flat Earth beneath a star-spangled sky, made shrewd but uninformed guesses about its origin.

My original plan was that this book should be an outline history of geology; I am very grateful to the publishers for their insistence that I should widen its scope. 'Science is one' and geology is intimately related not only to other branches of knowledge, from astronomy to nuclear physics, but to history and religious thought.

I hope, too, to show the debt that we owe to the great thinkers of past and modern times who strove, sometimes in the face of hostility and even of physical peril, to throw light upon the nature of this surprising world.

I.O.E.

Published by The Hamlyn Publishing Group Ltd
London · New York · Sydney · Toronto
Hamlyn House, Feltham, Middlesex, England
In association with Sun Books Pty. Ltd. Melbourne.

Reprinted 1973

ISBN 0 600 00092 3
Photoset by BAS Printers Limited, Wallop, Hampshire
Colour separations by Schwitter Limited, Zurich
Printed in Holland by Smeets, Weert

CONTENTS

EARLY AND CLASSICAL TIMES

Minerals and man

If we are asked which of the Earth's mineral products has been most useful to man we might suggest iron or coal or oil. Yet in early times flint was far more useful than any of these substances.

Long before metal was smelted, our ancestors made tools and hunting implements of stone. Indeed, subhuman fore-runners of man picked up flint pebbles and knocked them roughly into shape. The earliest artifacts are so crudely made that they might have been formed naturally, but later types were obviously chipped artificially, though the creatures who made them differed in some respects from ourselves.

The very earliest implements made by 'true' men are more elaborately shaped and more specialized, and great improve-

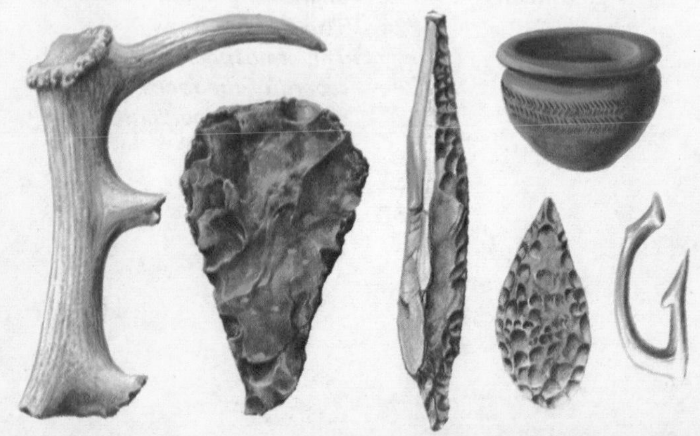

ments were later devised in their manufacture. Carefully chipped, not polished, into shape, they include axe heads and spear heads, scrapers, chisels, borers, and knives. They served not only for hunting but also for working in bone, reindeer horn, and wood. Later, a more efficient way of shaping flint was discovered – polishing. This enabled arrowheads to be provided with barbs, holes to be bored in stone, and a variety of other implements to be manufactured. These implements included sickle blades, for the age of polished stone was also that of corn growing, as well as of many other arts which made a civilized settled life possible.

Only in recent times was the usefulness of metal discovered; then flint was superseded, first by bronze, then by iron, and then by steel, the material basis of our modern mechanized world. All these metals, and many other raw materials, are derived from the mineral products of the Earth.

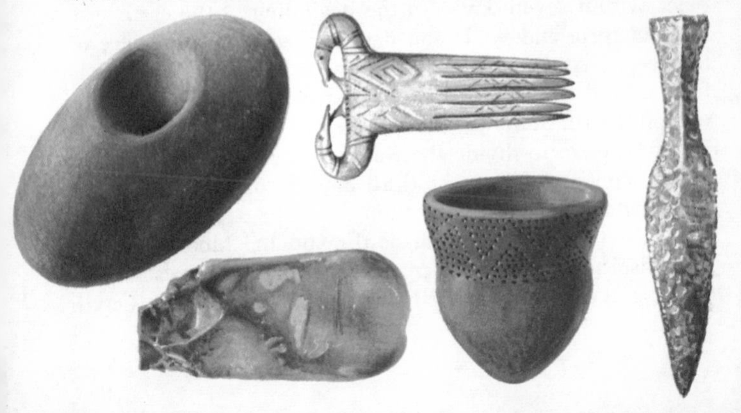

The Biblical account of Creation

The development of geological science was long swayed by the account of the world's creation given in the first chapter of the Book of Genesis; it was then regarded as essential that all its theories should harmonize with this account.

Here the creation of heaven and earth is described as taking place within seven days. 'In the beginning ... the earth was without form and void; and darkness was upon the face of the deep.... And God said, "Let there be light": and there was light ... and God divided the light from the darkness.' That was on the first day. On the second day God created a firmament, Heaven, to divide the waters below from those above the firmament; and on the third day the dry land appeared and was clothed with vegetation.

On the fourth day God made the Sun and Moon and 'the stars also'; on the fifth He created the marine animals and the birds; and on the sixth the land animals. It was on this sixth

'Thus the heavens and the earth were finished, and all the host of them.'

day, too, that, as a separate act of creation, He made man in His own image.

'And on the seventh day God ... rested.'

In this narrative, 'the heavens' are mentioned in so far as they are of importance to the world and to man; the Sun and Moon are made 'to give light upon the earth' and to act as a natural timepiece, 'to divide the day from the night: and ... for signs, and for seasons, and for days, and years. ...'.

Here there is no mention of the Earth's internal structure or mineral products. In Genesis II, however, there is a reference to gold and to some semi-precious stones. Later in Genesis comes another narrative to which geological theory was long expected to conform: 'Noah's Flood'. Sent to punish man for his sinfulness, it is described as covering the whole Earth and as destroying almost the whole of mankind and all of animal life – the only survivors being Noah and his family and the living creatures that he took with him into the Ark.

Other accounts of creation

The Biblical narratives of the Creation and the Flood are now regarded as based upon older legends of Babylonian origin. These, however, are fantastic and naïve, and abound in 'gods' and monsters. Only the god of Babylon, Marduk, is able to overcome the monster Tiamat, a sort of personification of the watery deep. In the Babylonian story of the Flood, too, numerous gods are implicated and they seem to be scared at the magnitude of the disaster.

Though the Egyptian creation story is very different, it is just as fantastic. The god of the air, Shu, is represented as separating the sky-goddess, Nut, from the earth-god, Geb – much as, in the later Greek mythology, the sky is kept from falling by the support of the giant Atlas.

In those early civilizations religion and science mingled, and the priests were the first astronomers. The Egyptians believed that the sun was rolled across the sky by the beetle-god Khepri, but study of the stars enabled them to

A fantasy depicting the Egyptian theory of creation

measure the length of the year, knowledge essential to any agricultural people. The Babylonians confused the planets with the gods after which they were named, but their observations enabled them to predict the eclipses.

The Earth was then thought of as being generally flat beneath the sky vault. Across this vault moved the Sun and Moon and the stars – including five 'wandering stars', the planets, which, unlike the other stars, had bewildering movements of their own.

The Creation narrative in Genesis clearly presupposes the same belief in a flat Earth beneath a vault-like sky. Its purpose is not scientific, but religious; instead of a fantastic assortment of gods it extols the One God, the Creator of Heaven and Earth. This singleness of purpose enabled it to sway the human mind as none of the other creation stories could have done. It is hard to imagine that any of them could influence scientific thought as did the Biblical accounts of the Creation and the Flood.

The shape of the Earth

As the travellers of those early civilizations made long journeys across the sea, they encountered some inexplicable and disquieting facts.

When they sailed from the land the coast they had left seemed to sink into the sea, and as they neared another shore it seemed to rise gradually from the waves. When another vessel approached them, her topmasts and sails came into sight before her hull became visible.

Not only did the Sun and Moon and stars seem to rise from below the eastern horizon and sink below that of the west; in regions far to the north, or south, of the homeland the noonday sun was unusually low, or unusually high, in the heavens, and some of the old familiar stars were lost to view

When an observer on the shore watches a ship that is approaching him, he is able to see the slender top-masts long before the rest of the ship. The massive hull of the ship is still hidden by the 'bulge' of the Earth.

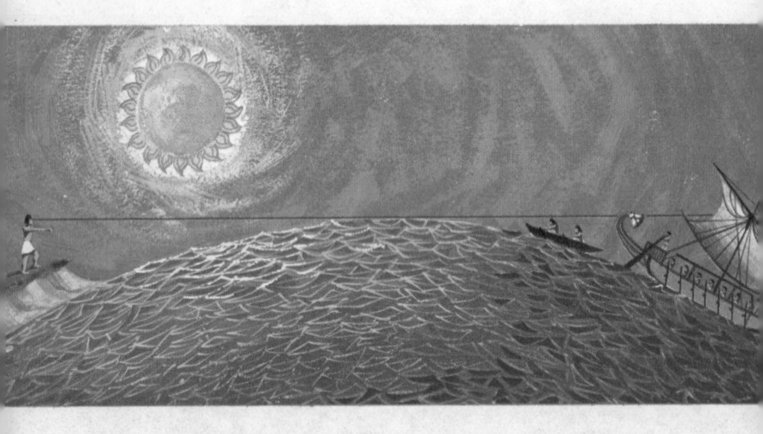

and other stars hitherto unknown appeared in the sky. A star, familiar to sailors in the Mediterranean but out of sight from Britain, is Canopus, one of the brightest in the sky.

Seeking to understand these facts, some of the seafarers and the thinkers whom they consulted must at last have inferred that the sea, apparently so level, has a slight bulge –

Seen from one country, the sun may be overhead, while from another, it appears some distance above the horizon.

and so too has the land, though the inequalities of its surface made this harder to realize. So they reached a surmise which for a time must have seemed completely absurd. The more the facts were studied, however, the more plausible this became, until it could at last be accepted as true. The Earth is not, as it seems, a flat surface beneath the vault of heaven, but a sphere surrounded by the far larger sphere of the sky.

Those who first formed this theory may have decided to keep it secret and to discuss it only with trusted colleagues without letting it be more widely known; to announce it publicly might invite not only ridicule but persecution. Thinkers have more recently incurred obloquy for ideas far less subversive than this. Clashing as it did with the religious beliefs of the time, it might have seemed not merely absurd but blasphemous.

Hence we do not know by whom, or among what peoples, it was first realized that the Earth is not flat, but round.

Astronomy becomes a science

There were, however, people who welcomed new theories and were ready to believe not only that the Earth is a sphere but that it actually moves – the Greeks. Some Greek philosophers, for mystical reasons, surmised that, like the Sun and the Moon and the planets and like a 'Counter Earth' invisible to ourselves, the Earth travels round a 'Central Fire'. Others believed that it rotates on its axis and circles around the Sun.

Most, however, thought this improbable. While realizing that the Earth is a sphere, they regarded it as standing motionless at the centre of the sky, with the heavenly bodies revolving round it. The stars move steadily, completing one circuit every day, but the motion of the Sun and Moon varies and that of the planets is irregular. At times they pause and then for a short period they actually move backward before again travelling onward.

An attempt to explain this was made in the fourth century BC by Aristotle. Believing that the 'natural' motion of the heavens is in perfect circles at steady speeds, he explained the seeming irregularities as being due to a number of hollow transparent spheres that surround the Earth; though each moves steadily they rotate at different speeds and some are slightly askew. As it takes the combined action of three or

Simplified view of Aristotle's conception of concentric transparent spheres, centred on the Earth and surrounded by the sphere containing the stars, by which the Sun, Moon and planets were moved

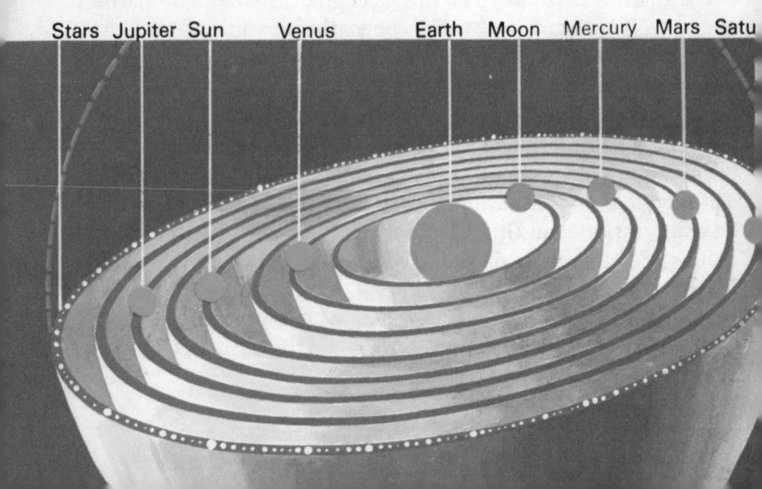

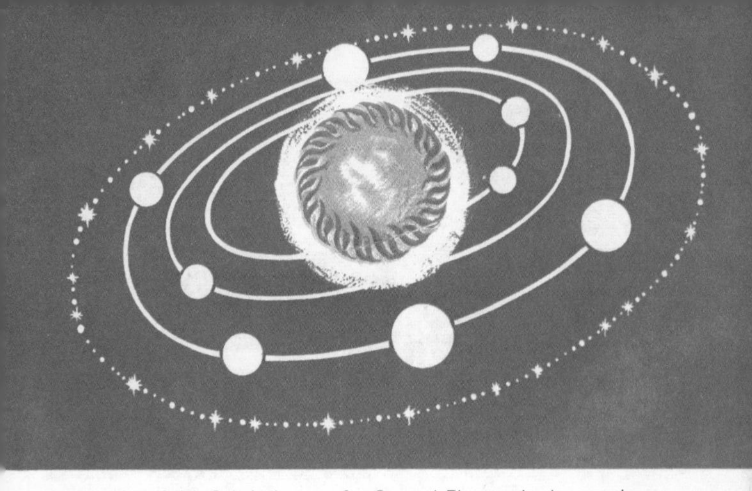

Illustration of the Greek theory of a Central Fire motionless at the heart of the universe with Earth and Counter Earth and heavenly bodies revolving around it

four of them to move one planet, they make that planet's motions seem irregular.

Founded in 332 BC by Alexander the Great, Alexandria in Egypt became a great centre of scientific research. Here the stars were catalogued and the year measured more accurately than before. Here the Greek astronomer Aristarchus, who believed that the Earth moves round the Sun, tried to measure the distance between them. He announced that the Sun is about nineteen times further away than the Moon, and about seven times broader and three hundred times more bulky than the Earth.

Such views were doubted, however, and in the second century AD Ptolemy suggested a theory less complicated than Aristotle's. Agreeing that the Earth is motionless with the heavens circling round it, he explained that the centres of the 'epicycles' in which the Sun and planets move are not fixed, but move in larger circles round the Earth.

Though far from simple, this Ptolemaic System was generally accepted, and centuries later it was adopted by Moslem and Christian thinkers. Nothing in it contradicted the Biblical narrative of Creation which, after all, nowhere states explicitly that the Earth is flat.

Part of an early Greek world map showing the ocean stream

The Earth and the 'inhabited world'

The Greek geographers made a distinction between the planet Earth and what they called 'the inhabited world', the home of man. Their knowledge of this was limited; for the regions beyond the western end of the Mediterranean they had to depend on surmise and on 'travellers' tales', the semi-legendary accounts of some early voyages.

Homer's *Odyssey*, for example, recounts the perils that the Greek hero Odysseus, or Ulysses, faced while returning from the siege of Troy: Scylla, a fearsome monster bristling with clutching arms, and Charybdis, which alternately gulped down and vomited up the sea; the Cyclops, one-eyed giants who pelted passing vessels with rocks; and the Sirens, whose song lured those who heard it to their doom.

These legends had a factual basis embellished by a poet intent on making his hearers' flesh creep. Scylla was an octopus unexpectedly seen by some panic-stricken mariner, and Charybdis was simply the Atlantic tides, strange and fearsome to seamen from the tideless Mediterranean. Cyclops was a volcano, towering up like a fiery-eyed giant and erupting masses of lava, and the Sirens were the seabirds with their plaintive cries.

The early geographers explained that the 'golden fleece'

for which the hero Jason and the Argonauts went in quest was a poetic description of the sheep's pelt used to trap gold dust swept down by a mountain stream. They could hardly have imagined, however, that the 'clashing rocks', said to have imperilled the good ship *Argo*, recalled a voyage among the northern ice-bergs! As Colchis, where the fleece was found, was supposed to be somewhere near the Black Sea, their ideas of geography must have been vague.

Such legends apart, these ideas were straightforward and simple. The early maps show the 'inhabited world' as one great land mass, partly divided by the Mediterranean and completely surrounded by an encircling 'ocean stream'; of the regions beyond this nothing was known.

Jason's golden fleece may well have been a sheepskin used when sifting for gold dust.

Pytheas found sailing in the North Atlantic impossible. He did not realize that the 'curdled sea' was the edge of the Arctic ice floes.

Early voyages of exploration

Some of the early voyages are better substantiated. In about 600 BC Pharoah Necho entrusted some Phoenician seamen with the circumnavigation of Africa. Taking three years over the voyage, they cruised down the Red Sea, rounded the Cape – where, to their amazement, they saw that the noon Sun was in the north – and returned by way of the Mediterranean to Egypt.

The Phoenicians traded regularly with the 'Tin Islands' (Britain), and in the sixth century BC their captain Himilco went off course through the Atlantic, where he encountered sea monsters and tracts of seaweed. If he had reached the Sargasso Sea, then by sailing further westwards he might have discovered America!

At about the same time another Phoenician, Hanno of Carthage, led a colonizing expedition down the west coast of Africa. Having founded settlements in Morocco and elsewhere, he pushed on further south, to the mouth of the Senegal and an island off Sierra Leone. After some alarming experiences, including a brush with some 'hairy people'

In the sixth century BC, Hanno of Carthage sailed to western Africa and encountered 'hairy people', probably chimpanzees.

(probably chimpanzees), his supplies ran out and he had to return to Carthage.

About a century later the Greek traveller Herodotus set out to investigate the known world, including Babylon and Persia, southern Italy and Egypt. His travels enabled him to compile his famous *History*, full of fascinating information about the ancient world. Though he recorded the 'travellers' tales' that reached him, he dealt with them critically; for example, he said he could find no evidence for the world-surrounding ocean stream.

In the fourth century BC the Greek scientist Pytheas of Massalia sailed northwards up the Atlantic to Britain, whose climate he described as 'extremely chilly'. Beyond another country further north, he added, was a region in which travel was impossible; there was a 'curdled sea', a 'sea-lung', which heaved as though some monster were breathing beneath the waves. His contemporaries ridiculed this, but the modern explorer Nansen regarded it as a graphic description of the ice sludge that forms along the edge of the Arctic ice floes.

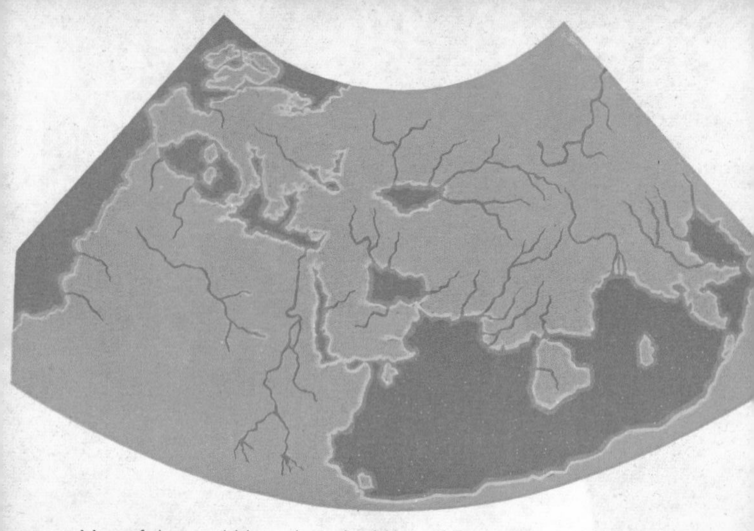

Map of the world based on the ideas of Ptolemy

Geography becomes a science

Alexander's expedition across Asia into India also contributed to geographical knowledge, and it was in the city he founded, Alexandria, that Eratosthenes succeeded in measuring the Earth in the third century BC. Learning that at Syene (the modern Aswan), which is due south of Alexandria, the noon sun is directly overhead and casts no shadow on midsummer day, he chose that day to measure the angle of slope of the noon shadows in his own city. Finding that they were roughly $7\frac{1}{2}°$ out of the vertical, he inferred that the distance between the two places (about 5000 *stadia*) was $7\frac{1}{2}°$ of the Earth's circumference. This showed its circumference to be about 250,000 *stadia* or about 24,670 miles – amazingly near the now accepted figure of just over 24,900 miles!

When mapping the known world he measured distances along two perpendicular lines, running north to south and east to west through the island of Rhodes. This device was later developed by Hipparchus, who suggested that a map of the world should be covered by a network of similar lines.

Strabo, who in the first century AD tried to use this method, realized that it is impossible to represent a spherical world on a flat surface. What was needed was not a map, but a globe at least ten feet across. Such a globe was said to have been made by Crates, librarian of Pergamum in Asia Minor. Knowledge of the world was meantime extended further by two daring traders: Hippalus found a new route across the Arabian Sea to India, and Alexander found a similar route across the Bay of Bengal to Malaya.

In the second century AD the astronomer Ptolemy included on a map of the world all the geographical information then available. His map has serious inaccuracies. It greatly overestimated the breadth of the 'inhabited world' and represented Africa as being linked to the south of China by land, with the Indian Ocean as an inland sea. None the less it was a great cartographic advance, and Ptolemy's map – and, indeed, its very inaccuracies – had a far-reaching influence on subsequent history.

Eratosthenes calculated the circumference of the Earth by measuring the angles of shadows.

Early ideas of geology

Compared with the advances they made in other branches of science, and especially in astronomy, the Greek thinkers' backwardness in geology is surprising. This may have been due to several reasons. Whereas, then as now, the 'heavens' were revered as the realm of divine beings, the 'underworld' on the other hand was distrusted as the abode of some rather sinister spirits.

The Greek philosophers, who valued knowledge and especially mathematical knowledge for its own sake, tended to despise its practical applications as servile – and in those early days the mines were chiefly worked by slaves. Those who had first-hand experience of the Earth's mineral products, the mining engineers and the metallurgists, may also have preserved their knowledge jealously as a trade secret.

The philosophers were, however, curious about the scenery and especially about its more impressive features, and they abandoned the old fables about 'the gods' for matter-of-fact views. Herodotus commented sarcastically that the gorge of Tempe, which allows the waters enclosed in the Plain of Thessaly to escape to the sea, might have been cleft open by a kindly god, if gods are responsible for earthquakes for anyone could see it was caused by an earthquake! And Strabo, writing years later, attributed it to an earthquake and did not mention the gods at all.

Even the 'master of them that know', Aristotle, who laid the foundations of biology, gave somewhat perfunctory attention to geology. He thought that the Sun's heat makes the Earth give off not only 'moist exhalations' that condense to form the clouds, but also 'dry exhalations' that produce thunder and lightning and the 'thunder bolts' cast on to the Earth with great violence. Between them they develop two varieties of material within the Earth, the metals and the non-metallic minerals. These were also made, he believed, by the action of the rays given off by the Sun and by the other heavenly bodies.

Peasants bowing to Mount Olympus while an impassive philosopher makes notes. The peaks of Olympus were supposed to be the throne of Zeus and the seats of the gods.

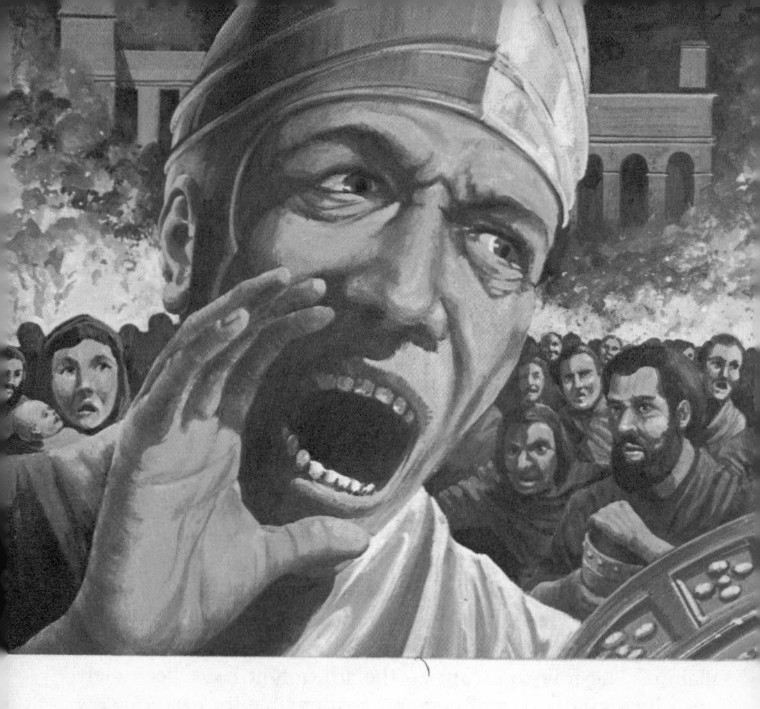

Theories of the Earth's structure

Appalled at such disasters as earthquakes and volcanoes, the Greek philosophers sought to explain them. Aristotle believed that they were caused by the action of immense volumes of air. Air, rushing into the Earth's interior through fissures in its surface, accumulated in immense subterranean cavities. far larger than what are commonly regarded as caves. When its pressure grew too great, the overstressed air rushed out, displacing the rocks with a violent uproar and making the solid ground tremble. It was even suggested that the air could be forced into the Earth through crevices beneath the sea, its retreat being cut off by the water. For this reason, it was thought, earthquakes usually occur in regions near the shore; hence the god of the sea was traditionally known as 'Poseidon, Shaker of Earth'.

The Earth was indeed compared, not fancifully but mystically, to the human body, traversed throughout its whole extent by channels analogous to the veins. As it was regarded

On 24 August 79 AD Vesuvius erupted and buried Pompeii under pumice and ash. Many of the 20,000 population perished.

as self-evident that a completely empty space is impossible, these channels were thought to be full of air or water, and in them huge uncouth animals might live.

These channels might also contain fire, for the rushing air was thought to get so intensely hot at times that it burst into flame, emerging at the surface as a volcano. Here was another vestige of traditional beliefs, for the volcanoes had once been thought to act as vents for the forges of the god Hephaestus, blacksmith and armourer to the gods, later known as Vulcan.

One volcanic eruption is notorious. In 79 AD the Italian city of Pompeii had hardly been rebuilt after a disastrous earthquake when it was overwhelmed; what had hitherto seemed like an ordinary mountain, Vesuvius, suddenly became a volcano. A Roman philosopher, the Elder Pliny, hastened to the scene, to help organize rescue work and to study the eruption. Overcome by the clouds of vapour and volcanic dust, he gave his life for humanity and science.

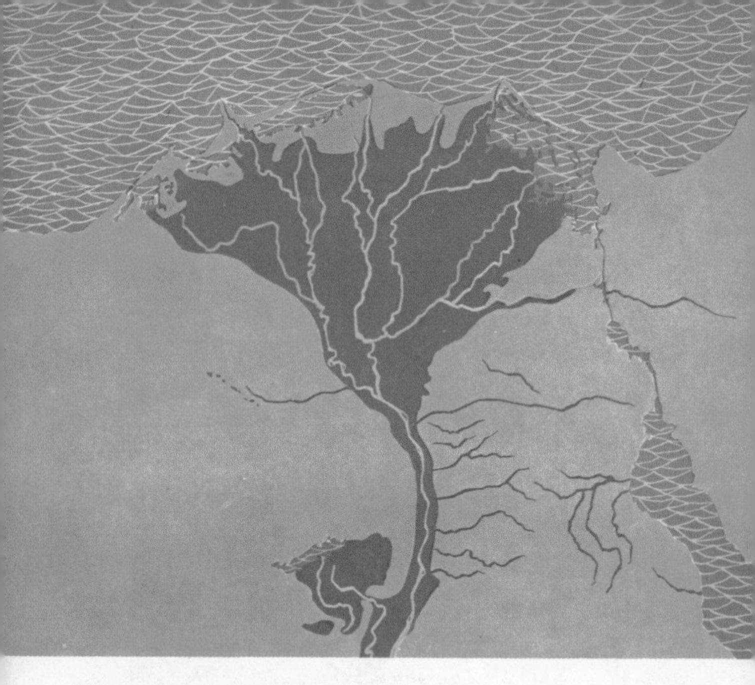

The inconstant Earth

Streams and rivers perplexed the philosophers, who could not imagine where all the water came from. Perhaps because he lived in a limestone region of abundant springs, Aristotle thought that the bulk of it came not from the rain or the melting of the mountain snows but from within the Earth. As he said, 'We do not call water that flows anyhow a river, even if there is a great deal of it, but only if it comes from a spring.'

Springs, he believed, were fed partly by water that had seeped into the ground, partly from the air which had been driven in by atmospheric pressure, and partly from some unspecified source deeper underground. He seems to have regarded mountains as a sort of waterlogged sponge.

The Roman author Seneca declared that although rainfall might swell a river's volume and even produce a torrent, it could not maintain a constant flow, and he suggested that the Earth itself might actually be transformed into water.

The Greek thinkers did however realize the action of rivers

in transporting and depositing silt. Herodotus called the fertile plain of Lower Egypt 'the gift of the Nile', and Aristotle asserted that the whole region had once been covered by the sea, the silt brought down by the Nile having first made the water shallow and then converted it into marshes that had gradually dried up. Elsewhere, too, he inferred, rivers had been born and perished, and the sea itself had undergone similar changes, so that a region is not always water or always dry land but changes its condition in the course of time. This belief that what is now dry land had once been under the sea was confirmed by the occurrence of former sea shells in regions now inland.

Yet instead of a wealth of careful observations that could form the basis of acute theories, knowledge of the Earth's surface was limited to a few casually-noticed and misunderstood facts and to some ingenious guesses many of which were wide of the mark. Unlike astronomy and geography, geology did not become a science in classical times.

(*Left*) the Nile Delta. Egypt's fertile soil is a thin layer of silt brought down from Ethiopia. (*Below*) a medieval idea of the origin of rivers.

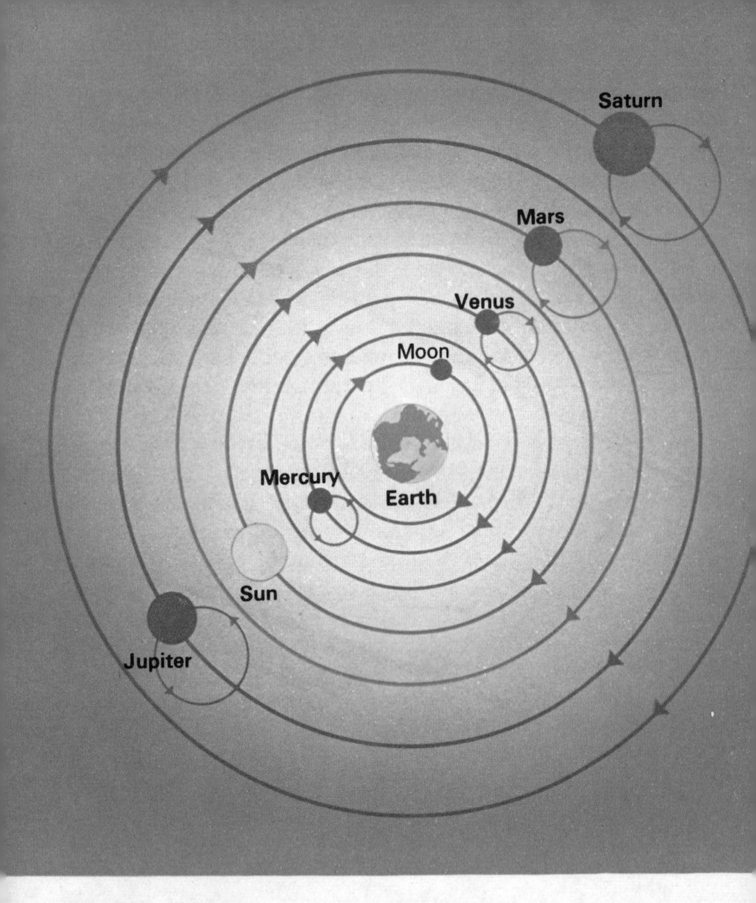

THE MIDDLE AGES AND THE RENAISSANCE

'When it was dark'

Scanty as was the geological lore acquired in classical times, much even of this was forgotten during the 'Dark Ages'. It was replaced by some curious speculations regarding the 'generation of stones', the manner in which rocks, minerals and jewels had come into existence.

A few stones, for example, are hollow with small pebbles inside them – how natural to assume that the inner stone was literally the offspring of the outer one, that the latter had, so to speak, given birth. How natural to deduce that some stones have a sex, being either male or female, or that stones can literally 'grow' within the Earth!

As 'stones' do actually form, with painful results, within the human body, it was natural to infer that they are likewise produced within the bodies of animals. Such stones were thought to have valuable properties. After killing a serpent, a stag was supposed to weep copiously, its tears congealing into a stone; this stone was thought to be an antidote against poison. Even more highly esteemed was the bezoar stone, believed to form within the stomach of some oriental goat-like animal; it was so highly valued as a protection against not only poison but the plague that it sold for as much as ten times its weight in gold. A trade in spurious bezoar stones developed and a Fellow of the Royal Society thought it worth while to carry out a systematic enquiry, the natural result of which was to 'debunk' the whole legend.

On the other hand the Ptolemaic theory of astronomy was still accepted. The Earth was regarded as a globe, motionless at the centre of the Universe. Around it moved concentric 'spheres' carrying, in order, the Moon, Mercury, Venus, the Sun, Mars, Jupiter and Saturn. Beyond this another sphere carrying the stars was rotated by yet another, the 'Prime Mover'; and beyond this, and indeed beyond space and time, was the 'Tenth Heaven', the abode of the Almighty. This view summarized the observed facts admirably, but its complications made it hard to forecast heavenly movements.

(*Left*) Ptolemaic theory of astronomy. (*Below*) illustration of the medieval bezoar stone and the goat-like animal from which it was supposed to come

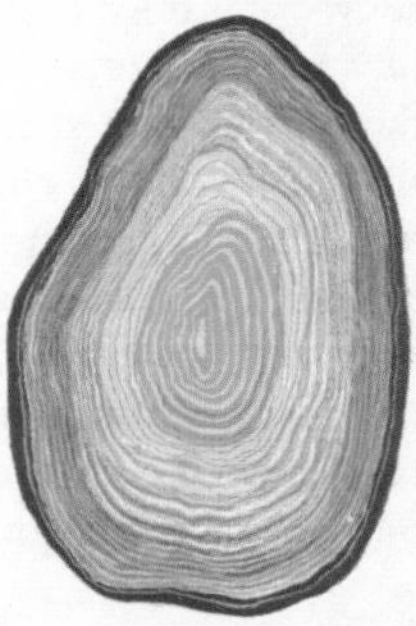

Journeys to east and west

About the fifth century AD some adventurous Irish monks voyaged out into the unknown in search of 'the Island of the Blessed', an Earthly paradise believed to lie towards the sunset. Their traditional leader was St Brendan, and attempts have been made to reconstruct the factual basis of the legends associated with him.

Sailing 'by guess and by God', his monks are said to have reached 'the island of sheep, where it is always summer', possibly Madeira. They entered a 'clogged sea' resembling the sea lung described by Pytheas, and saw a cloud-capped column made of clear crystal but as hard as stone, evidently an iceberg. They approached a desolate shore reeking of sulphur where demon forges seemed to be at work underground. A 'giant blacksmith' on the coast stoked up his furnace until the sea boiled, and pelted his visitors with lumps of burning slag, but thanks to St Brendan's prayers they got safely away. They had been appalled at the sight of an Icelandic volcano. Thanks to their heroism, 'St Brendan's Isle' long stirred the imagination of Europe. Although mythical, and perhaps the result of a mirage, it helped to stimulate exploration of the Atlantic.

Some centuries later the Vikings, who had been 'island hopping' westwards from Norway by way of the Orkneys, the Shetlands, the Faroes, and northern Scotland and Ireland, reached and colonized Iceland. From there, Eric the Red sailed on to Greenland, and in about 1000 AD his son Leif Erisson, cruising still further westwards, discovered a hitherto unknown land, that he called 'Vineland the Good'. This discovery of America gave rise to traditions which further stimulated exploration.

Equally stimulating was Marco Polo's exploit when, in about 1275, he reached Pekin after crossing Asia. His descriptions of the wealth and wonders of Cathay (China) greatly encouraged land travel and trade, as did his mention of a large island, hitherto unheard-of in Europe. This was Cipangu, known to its inhabitants as Nippon, to us as Japan.

Vikings encounter Red Indians, and (*left*) St Brenden and his monks are appalled at the sight of an Icelandic volcano

Systematic exploration

The eastern lands vaguely called 'the Indies' were difficult to reach. Whether overland across Asia or by sea through the Mediterranean and then, after a 'portage' over the Isthmus of Suez, down the Red Sea and across the Indian Ocean, the routes were full of peril. Something safer and more expeditious was needed.

In the fifteenth century Prince Henry of Portugal – Henry the Navigator – organized a systematic exploration of the West African coast. Here the limit of navigation was supposed to be Cape Bojador; beyond this, it was believed, the currents and trade winds, and above all the heat, made progress impossible. Henry had great difficulty in finding seamen bold enough to try.

At last he succeeded, and in 1434 Cape Bojador was rounded by Gil Eannes. Their fears overcome, the Portuguese pushed further and further southwards. In 1487 Bartholomew Diaz rounded the Cape of Good Hope and ten years later Vasco da Gama reached India by sea around Africa.

Meanwhile an Italian seaman, Christopher Columbus, had

World globe of Behaim, a German geographer. It was completed in the year Columbus discovered America (*opposite*), (1492), and is supposed to illustrate his geographical ideas.

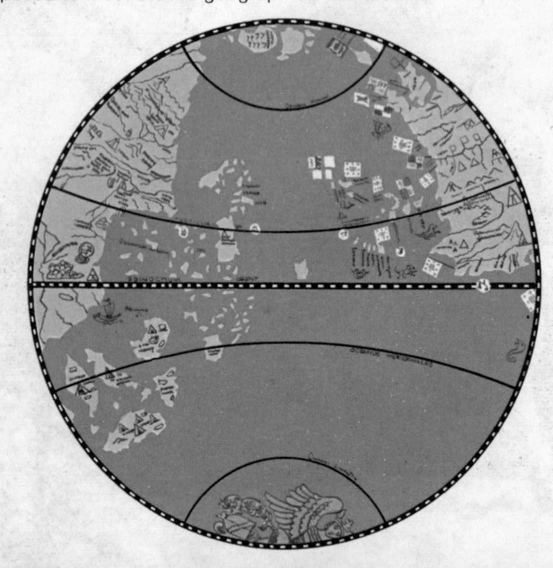

suggested reaching the Indies by a novel route not eastwards but westwards across the Atlantic. After much difficulty, he at last induced the Spanish monarchy to support his venture. With three small ships he sailed westwards, and in 1492 he reached what he mistook for the Indies and claimed them for the Spanish Crown. Then the amazed geographers realized that what Columbus had reached was not Asia but a land, hitherto unknown; it was later named America.

The maritime people of Europe were naturally anxious to exploit America's wealth. So, to prevent disputes, in 1494 Pope Alexander VI assigned all newly-discovered lands in the west of America to Spain and all in the east to Portugal. However, as the meridian he chose as the boundary was incorrect, Portugal received a sizeable area – now called Brazil – that the Pope had meant to allocate to Spain.

Needless to say, the other nations, Catholic or otherwise took little notice of the Pope's ruling. If they found an undefended region that seemed attractive, they annexed it.

The birth of geology

Civilization was now restored in Europe. The Arabs had studied the Greek and Latin records and made them known to Christendom; paper-making and printing enabled knowledge to be broadcast. The thinkers were studying the world around them: the sky, the sea – and the Earth.

They were especially perplexed by some strange objects found in the rocks, the things now called 'fossils' but then known as 'figured stones'. Partly on religious grounds, they were loath to believe that these were the actual remains of plants and animals. They attributed them to 'the influence of the stars', to a sort of 'trial run' of nature before it got down to the mass production of living creatures, or to 'freaks of Nature' as though Nature were playing a practical joke.

Among the thinkers who saw the absurdity of such notions was Leonardo da Vinci. After studying sea shells found in Italian rocks, he decided in 1508 that the creatures within them had actually lived on the sea floor and been buried in silt washed in rivers from the land. He pointed out that there are also tracts of gravel obviously consisting of material rounded and piled up by currents within the water.

One of the first systematic accounts of the figured stones was compiled in 1565 by the Swiss naturalist Conrad Gesner. Although it is illustrated so well that many of the fossils it dealt with are recognizable, they are classified simply by their appearance. Some, he pointed out, have geometric forms, some resemble earthly objects, animals or plants, some resemble the stars, and others must have 'fallen from the sky'.

The German mining engineer, George Bauer, also had an

(*Above*) the 'figured stones' that so baffled the thinkers.
(*Below*) renaissance mining technique

inkling of the nature of fossils. He has been called the 'Father of Mineralogy', for under a latinized version of his name, Agricola, he wrote in 1546 what is probably the first treatise on that science. Another of his works, *De Re Metallica*, published in 1556, describes and illustrates the technique of the mining industry in the sixteenth century.

The new astronomy

Now that their voyages spanned the world, seamen needed more than ever to be able to fix their position by the movements of the heavenly bodies and they increasingly found that the Ptolemaic system of astronomy was inadequate. Pondering over this problem, the Polish priest Copernicus was amazed to find that some of the Greek thinkers had considered it possible that Earth might circle round the Sun.

This assumption, he found, enabled those movements to be forecast more easily, and in 1543 he set out his 'Copernican System' in writing. But the publisher of his book, anxious to avoid conflict with the Roman Church, was careful to explain that it was merely a mathematical theory.

The Copernican system of astronomy

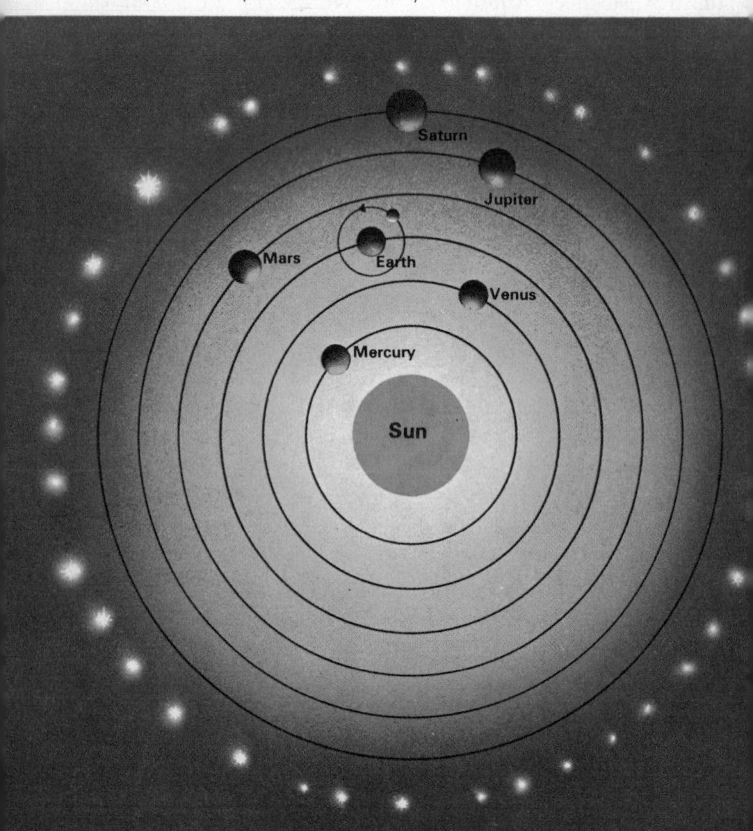

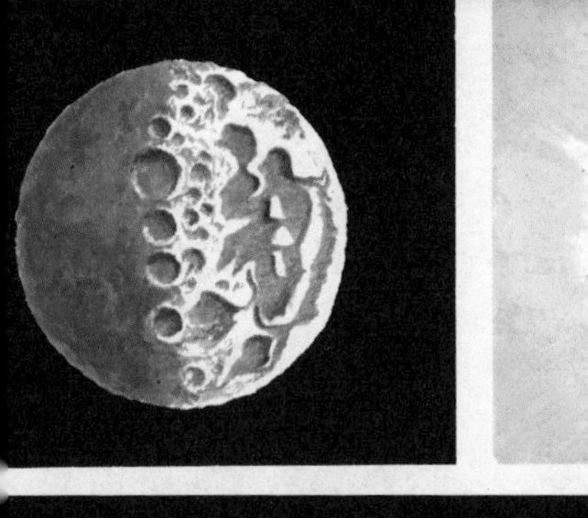
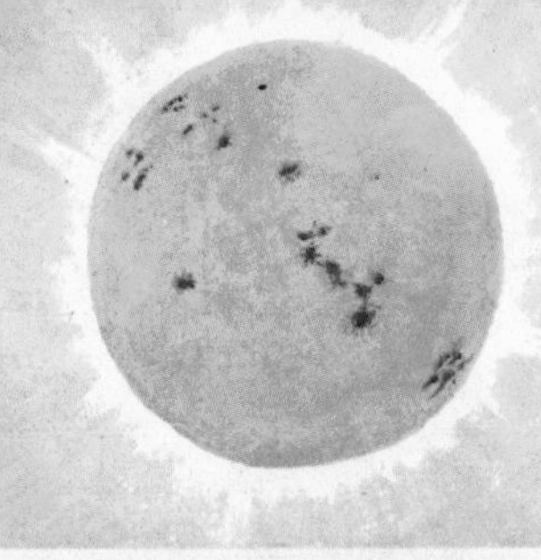
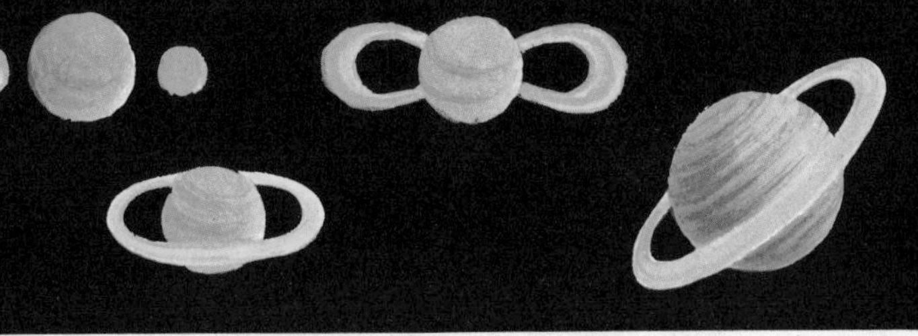

Galileo's discoveries; Moon craters, sunspots and Saturn's rings

Thinking it improbable, the Danish observational astronomer Tycho Brahe suggested a compromise: whereas the five planets travelled round the Sun, the Sun, taking the planets with it, travelled, like the Moon, round the Earth.

This compromise satisfied nobody, and the German mathematician Kepler used Tycho's careful observations in his attempts to explain the movements of the planets. He was able to show, in 1619, that each of the planets – including the Earth – travelled around the Sun in a simple curve, the flattened circle called an ellipse.

During that period, the early seventeenth century, the Italian physicist Galileo used the first astronomical telescope to study the sky. He discovered the mountains, craters and deserts, which he mistook for seas, on the Moon's surface, four of Jupiter's satellites, and Saturn's rings, which he mistook for companion planets. He was also the first to observe the sunspots. These discoveries, especially Jupiter's satellites, were hard to reconcile with the old Ptolemaic system and tended to confirm the Copernican system.

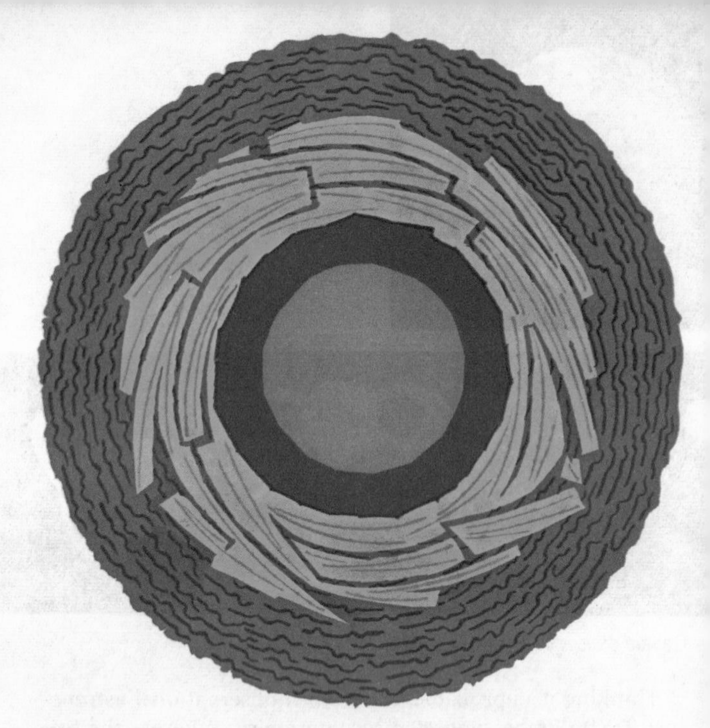

THE EARLY DEVELOPMENT OF GEOLOGY

Theories of the Universe

Although temporarily banned by the Roman Catholic Church as heretical, the Copernican system was such an advance on the Ptolemaic system that it was eventually accepted. It then formed the basis of several 'cosmologies', attempts to explain the origin of the world – or the Universe. Thus in 1644 Descartes attributed the movements of the heavenly bodies to vortices (swirls) in whatever it is that fills all space.

In protestant Britain, whose overseas trade demanded an accurate prediction of those movements, the New Astronomy was welcomed, and in 1686 Isaac Newton's Law of Gravitation gave it a sound theoretical basis. His work supplanted the vortice theory of Descartes, but that thinker had been happier in his view of the Earth's development. He believed that, together with the other planets, it had once been as intensely hot as the Sun, but that the Earth had gradually cooled sufficiently for its outer layers to become solid.

This view was carried further by Buffon, who in 1749 published his theory that the Earth and the other planets had formed part of the Sun until they had been torn from its surface and given their movement and spin by the shock of a comet. In 1778 he went into greater detail. Interpreting the biblical 'days' of Creation as periods of indeterminate length he regarded the Earth's history as divided into six great Epochs. He even tried to estimate their duration by calculations based on the rate of cooling of cast iron.

Inaccurate as his results were – necessarily, for they lacked an observational basis – they showed that thinkers were no longer tied down to a literal belief in the Biblical narrative of Creation. Thanks to the New Astronomy this and the Biblical account of Noah's Flood could be interpreted liberally, in a manner almost unthinkable in old pre-Copernican days.

Buffon's theory of the Earth's development (*opposite*). Originally molten and incandescent, it gradually cooled from the surface inward, so that while still intensely hot at its centre, its crust hardened and split to form the mountains and valleys and was surrounded by atmospheric vapours and steam. (*Below*) the gravitational pull of the Sun and Moon causes the Earth's tides. When both pull in line at new and full moon (*left*) the tides are higher. When they pull at right angles, counteracting one another, tides are lower.

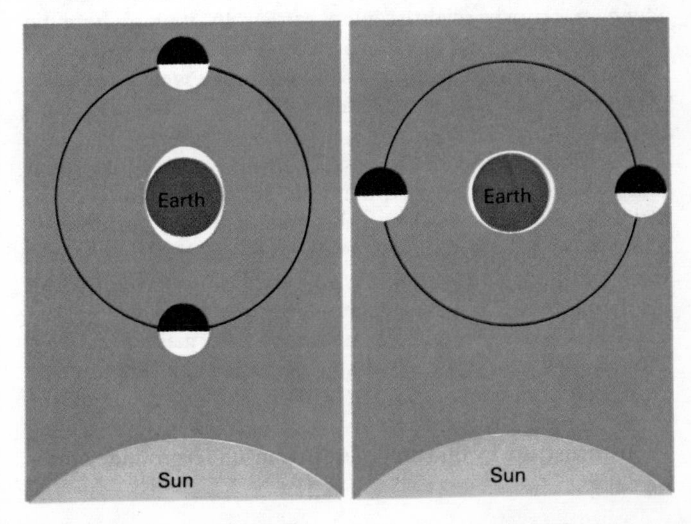

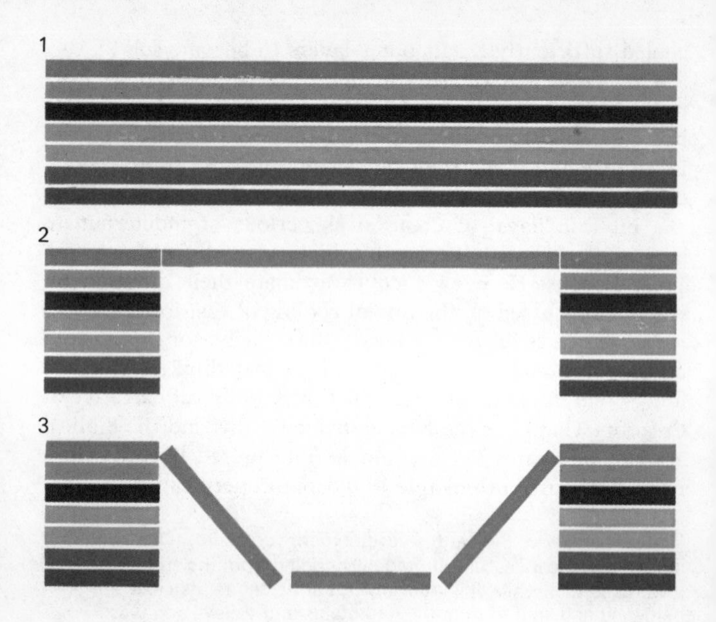

'Solids contained within a solid'

While some thinkers were devising cosmologies others were studying the rocks. Foremost among these men was Nicolas Steno, a Danish scientist who settled in Italy, where he became a bishop of the Roman Catholic Church. Before his conversion he published, in 1669. what may well be the first geological treatise. Its title refers to 'solids naturally contained within a solid'.

His solids included the fossils. Unlike most of his contemporaries, Steno decided that they are actually the remains of living creatures. Sea shells, he explained, had been buried about 4000 years previously by Noah's Flood, but the elephant teeth and bones dug out of the soil were those of the African elephants that Hannibal had brought over the Alps!

Discussing the origin of mountains, he maintained that though they had not existed since Creation they had not, as was then commonly thought, grown like trees out of the earth. Some he regarded as being of volcanic origin, having been thrust up by burning gases from underground, others

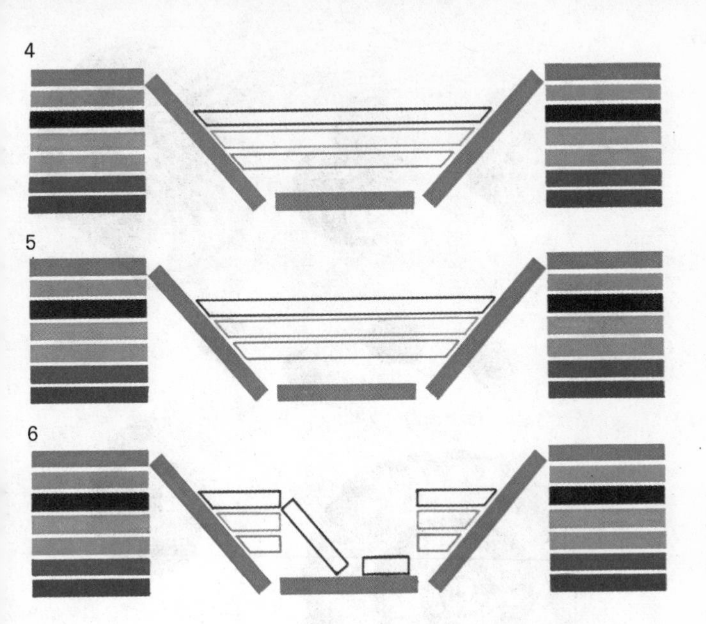

Six diagrams to illustrate Steno's treatise:

1. rock beds as originally deposited in horizontal layers
2. subterranean gulfs formed when the lower rock beds were destroyed by fire or water
3. mountains and valleys produced by the collapse of the upper rock beds
4. sandy rock beds (represented by outlines) deposited in the valleys by the sea
5. destruction of the lower sandy beds
6. hills and valleys produced by the collapse of the upper sandy beds

as being all was left when the material surrounding them had been washed away by water. Others again he attributed to a very different origin which he illustrated by diagrams, probably the first geological 'sections' ever to be produced.

Many of the rocks of Tuscany, he pointed out, were obviously hardened sediments, which were laid down under turbid waters. The fossils that they contain are additional evidence for this theory, illustrated diagrammatically above.

'Such a trivial thing as a rotten shell'

In England, as elsewhere, attempts to reconcile geology with Genesis regarded Noah's Flood as produced by the bursting of a subterranean abyss of water, accompanied perhaps by a deluge condensed from a comet. John Woodward, who studied the rocks systematically and bequeathed his splendid collection of fossils to Cambridge University, maintained (1695) that these fossils were relics of that Flood.

Other naturalists, even after studying and making drawings of these 'figured stones' still believed, however, that their resemblance to living creatures was purely coincidental. Their nature was among the subjects discussed by the Royal Society after it was granted its Charter by Charles II in 1662. Its Latin motto proclaims that 'we take no man's word for it', and its aim was to enquire into all branches of what was then called Natural Philosophy.

Robert Hooke, the Society's Curator of Experiments, whose theories may possibly have influenced those of Steno, was convinced that the 'figured stones' are precisely what they seem to be. He stated that they were either the petrified remains of living creatures or the impressions which their bodies have left in the rocks.

Noah's Flood, he was convinced, could not *possibly* account for them. Far greater catastrophies, including earthquakes so tremendous that they were accompanied by a displacement of the Earth's centre of gravity, must have repeatedly turned the sea into dry land and the land into sea. It must also have plunged southern England into the Torrid Zone and have completely destroyed many types of living creature.

Though it might be felt, he declared, that 'there is too much notice taken of such a trivial thing as a rotten shell ... yet ... these ... records of antiquity which Nature has left us' were far more reliable as a guide to the past than medals or coins. As for the notion that the fossils were 'freaks of Nature', he commented austerely that Nature was far too serious to indulge in something that could only be considered as pointless practical jokes.

Hooke's drawings of the fossils now known as ammonites, creatures akin to the *Nautilus* of tropical seas

Scheuchzer's relic of antediluvian man : a large salamander

Collectors' pieces

The disputes about the nature of 'figured stones' attracted public attention and made them popular as curios. It also induced naturalists to study them, most deciding that they formed concrete evidence of the reality of Noah's Flood.

The Swiss naturalist J. J. Scheuchzer, who accepted this view, expressed the pious hope that, God willing, some *human* evidence of the Flood would come to light in his own country. In 1726 he excitedly announced that a skeleton had been found of 'one of the infamous men who brought about the calamity of the Flood'. This relic is now displayed in a museum in Holland, where, however, it is labelled, following its identification by Cuvier, as the skeleton of a large salamander.

In 1708, Scheuchzer had written a geological fable. He described fossil fishes as protesting against this malicious denial of their real nature, a denial made by the descendants of the very sinners whose wickedness had been responsible for their entombment. In every detail, they pointed out, their structure was identical with that of living fish, and they praised the goodness of Providence in making them evidence of the Flood strong enough to convert even the most hardened of atheists.

Even more remarkable was a book by the German professor J. B. Beringer, also published in 1726, describing the extraordinary 'figured stones' to which his students had drawn his attention. They were adorned with a weird representation of a variety of objects, images of insects and birds, the Sun and the stars. His enthusiasm rose to its height when he found one of them inscribed, in Hebrew characters, with the Sacred Name of the Almighty.

Hardly had his book appeared when his discovery of a similar stone bearing his own name revealed the truth – his students, or maybe some malicious colleagues, had made him the victim of a cruel hoax. Thereafter he devoted himself to unavailing efforts to buy up and suppress all the copies of that wretched book, with the result, it is said, of ruining himself and shortening his life.

Beringer's 'figured stones', the results of a hoax

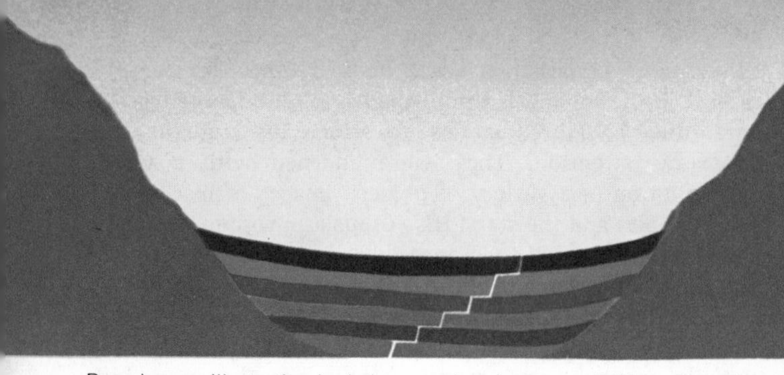

Based on an illustration by Lehmann showing two primitive mountains separated by a valley in which have accumulated a number of deposits washed down by Noah's Flood

The build of the rocks

During the eighteenth century several naturalists studied the build of their country's rocks from different points of view. John Strachey listed in 1719 and 1725 those of south-western England, from the coal up to the chalk, and pointed out that whereas the coal-bearing rocks slope more or less steeply, the rock beds above them lie almost horizontally across their edges.

Using terms that had been coined by the Abbé Anton Lazzaro Moro and were being adopted generally (and which indeed, though with more definite meanings, are still in use) Giovanni Arduino, in 1759, classified the rocks of northern Italy. He described as *primitive* or *primary* those mountains which 'practical' men value for their mineral wealth; his

Based on Lehmann's theory that the material washed down by the Flood from the primitive mountains accumulated in beds lining their slopes, which later form secondary mountains

secondary mountains consist of limestone and marble and contain few minerals but are rich in fossils; his *tertiary* formations include lower mountains and hills; and he also mentioned volcanic rocks and those formed of loose material washed down from the hill slopes.

A German savant, Johann Gottleb Lehmann, taught in 1756 that the primitive mountains, which include the highest peaks and mountain ranges, and whose roots extend far underground, were formed at the Creation and that, apart from a surface covering of earth, they had been left bare when the seas had been separated from the dry land. Noah's Flood, whose cause he thought to be inexplicable, had washed the earth from their surface, leaving them barren. It had deposited sediment in their valleys or against their sides, the fossils it contained being the remains of the creatures which had once inhabited the slopes of the primitive mountains. The lower mountains and the hills, he surmised, had been produced more recently by such minor catastrophies as local deluges and volcanoes.

His compatriot George Christian Füchsel observed in 1762 that certain rock beds contain their own special fossils. Just as fossil plants are characteristic of coal, so sea shells are typical of one formation and ammonites of another.

John Strachy's geological 'section' of an area in the Somerset coalfield: the seams of coal, which are represented by the black lines, had been broken and displaced by a fault.

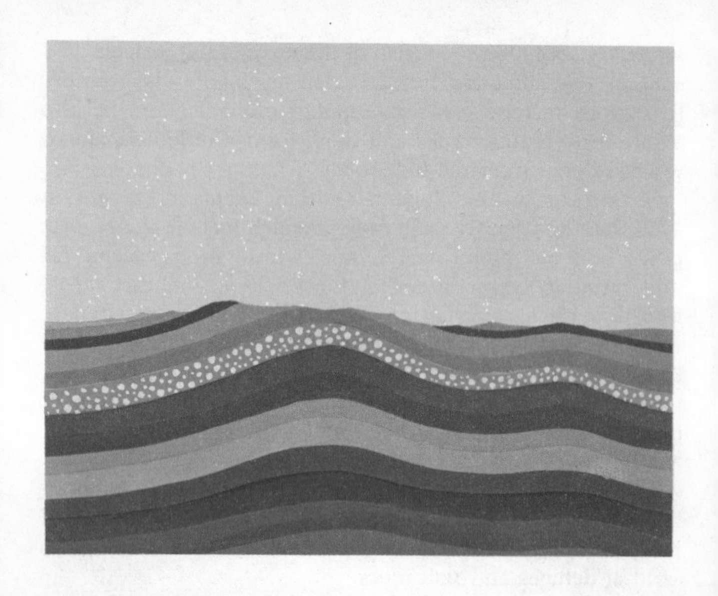

The earthquake year

The horror and alarm that earthquakes arouse have always been mingled with curiosity regarding their cause, and in the 1750s this problem was studied intensively by the Royal Society.

The decade, which had opened with the 'earthquake year' of 1750, in which several shocks had been experienced in western Europe and the south of England, had continued with further disturbances, culminating in the great convulsion that devastated Lisbon in 1755. It was in 1750, too, that a novel explanation of their cause had been suggested by W. Stukely – the newly-discovered force of electricity.

An older theory was expounded in great detail by the Reverend John Michell, who in 1761 published his 'conjectures concerning the cause ... and phenomena of earthquakes', with special reference to that of Lisbon.

Assuming, as had long been believed, that volcanoes were produced by the burning of inflammable material just beneath the Earth's surface, he inferred that the results might be much more far-reaching when the combustion took place

The Reverend John Mitchell's theory of the cause of earthquakes (*left*). Vapours accumulated in the gaps between the rock beds may be so tightly compressed that their movements or expansion produce an earthquake. (*Above*) inflammable vapours may break through a weak place in the surface rock, catch fire and break out as a volcano

deep underground. It would leave an empty space into which part of the overlying rocks would collapse, and the water which they contained would be converted into steam with explosive force. This would compress the roof of the whole cavity, and the release of the pressure would send a vibrations in all directions through the crust of the Earth, the shock-waves gradually dying away as they travelled further outwards. Michell ingeniously compared this action to the movement of a large carpet when its edge is raised and then slapped smartly down on the floor.

By noticing the direction and the speed in which the earth tremors moved, he explained, it should be possible not only to detect the centre where the shock took place but to estimate its depth underground. For the Lisbon earthquake, he ventured to make a guess of not less than a mile or a mile and a half, but not more than three miles, below the surface.

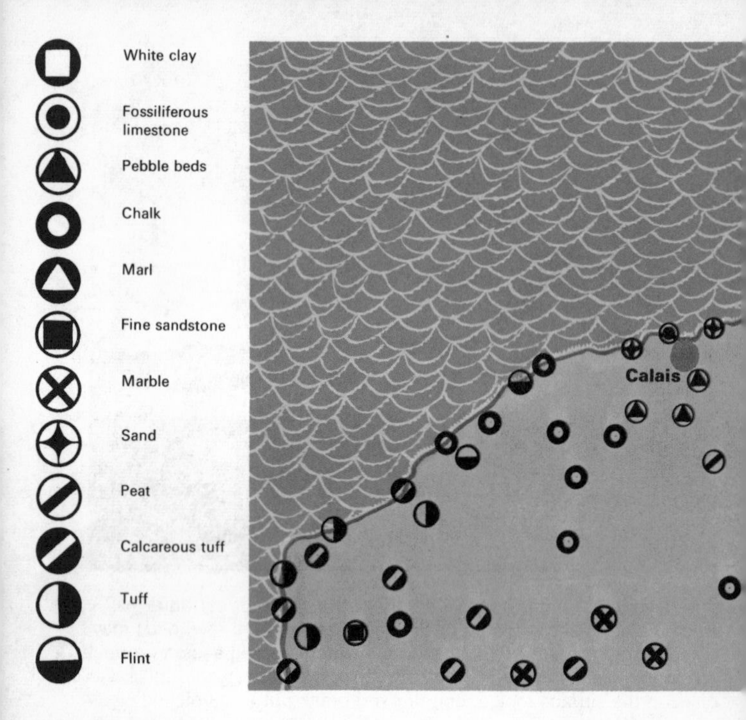

Early geological maps

In 1683 Martin Lister, a Fellow of the Royal Society, proposed 'a new sort of ... soile or mineral map', distinguishing by colours or shading the types of soil and rocks beneath them. He left its compilation to 'the industry of future times', so not until years later, in France, was such a map produced.

The French botanist Jean Étienne Guettard, who travelled widely collecting his specimens, noticed that every plant seemed always to grow in its own special soil. This interested him in minerals and rocks, and he realized that instead of occurring at random they seemed to be arranged in regular cross-country strips. In the Paris region there was a central oval of sand and gravel, with limestone and other building materials. Around this sandy strip was a marly strip consisting of limy clays. Outside this was a strip including marble and granite.

When indicating these strips on a map, Guettard saw that

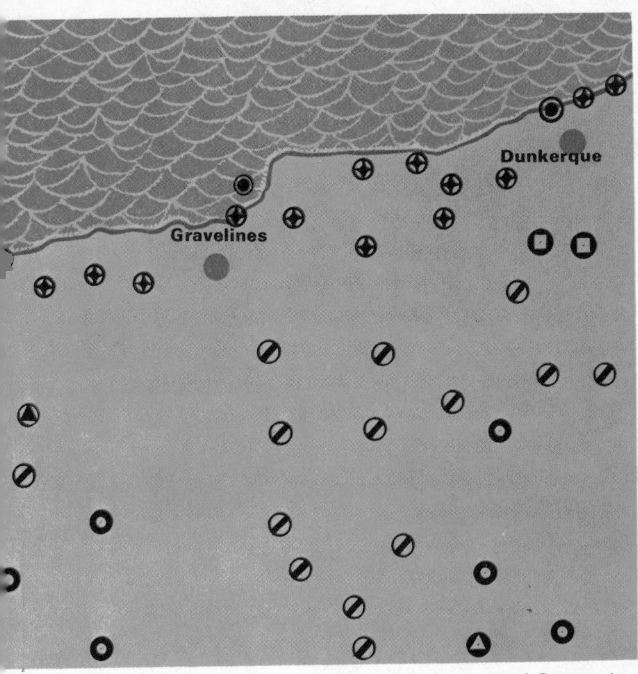

A geological map of northern France after the style of Guettard

they were cut short by the sea, and he inferred that they would continue on the opposite coast. Unable to visit England himself, he had to depend on books, so he mapped the rocks of southeast England less accurately than those of northwest France. He also prepared a similar small scale map for the whole of western Europe, including Iceland.

Though the French Academy welcomed these first geological maps and published them in 1751, Guettard was not satisfied. He wanted a larger-scale map of France on which to indicate its geology, and when the map was forthcoming he began setting it out in greater detail, accompanying his maps with illustrative cross-sections of the land. Before ill health made him relinquish his task to a colleague, he had travelled over 5000 miles and completed sixteen sheets of the map. Carried on by his successor, the whole map was produced in 1780.

Illustration of Guettard's fossils showing holes made by rock-boring animals or encrustations of sea mats

The ever-changing landscape

In the memoir that accompanied his maps and in his other works, Guettard illustrated a number of fossils and discussed their nature. Other naturalists might deny that 'figured stones' were the remains of living creatures but he, who had compared them with similar modern creatures, knew better.

He pointed out that both had suffered the same 'accidents'. Like shells of today, fossil shells were encrusted with smaller shells and barnacles; they were pierced with holes made by rock-boring animals; and they had been knocked about by waves. Here was convincing evidence of their real nature, evidence which showed too that the rocks in which they were found had once been beneath the sea.

Guettard found no difficulty in believing this, for he knew that changes had taken place in the landscape within living memory. As a child he had seen a strangely-shaped stone pinnacle which the countryfolk had called 'The Rock of the Good Virgin', yet within his own lifetime it had vanished completely while other rocks had appeared. These rocks looked as if they must have grown out of the ground, but all that had happened was that the material that had covered them had been washed away by rain.

It was rain, too, that had scoured the earth with deep channels and grooved the sides of hills. Landslips had been caused, not, as had been thought, by subterranean fires or blasts of air, but through the wearing away of underground rocks by water that had seeped down from the surface. Far greater was the destruction wrought on the coast by the sea.

Some of the material worn away by the rivers, Guettard explained, was deposited beside their course further downstream, so that the level of the valley floors was being slowly raised. The remainder, with the debris worn away from the coast by the waves, was swept out to sea and spread about on the sea floor. The very saltiness of the brine, he surmised, might be due to soluble material washed down from the land. As, however, the movements within the sea could have little effect at any depth, Guettard deduced that the submarine rocks revealed by the soundings, were the remains of mountains destroyed ages ago, and that it was their destruction which had produced the sand on the sea floor.

The extinct volcanoes of France

While mapping the rocks of Central France, Guettard noticed that some of the milestones were made of an unfamiliar black substance. When he was told that it came from 'Volvic' the name impressed him as significant, and he hastened to visit what he thought might be a centre of volcanic activity.

The nearer he approached it the more abundant this substance was, and when he reached the quarry from which it had come, he identified it as a hardened lava and was able to trace the very cone and crater from which it had flowed.

Though he had never visited an active volcano, his reading told him that the curved lines on some of the local rock resembled the 'ropy' structure of certain Vesuvian lavas and that the pumice so abundant in the neighbourhood was also of volcanic origin, having been frothed up while still molten by the eruptive gases. Cones and craters and other products of volcanic action were so numerous that he realized most of the Auvergne region must consist of extinct volcanoes.

Guettard believed that they were caused by oil, coal or pitch beneath the ground; when these fuels caught fire the result was an eruption. Hot springs nearby suggested that subterranean fires were still smouldering, and he was alarmed lest the local inhabitants should be imperilled. These people, however, were unperturbed and incredulous.

Another rock common in the district was basalt. Unlike certain other naturalists, Guettard did not regard basalt as volcanic but thought that it had crystallized out from some aqueous solution. On such questions the geologists of Europe were soon to quarrel bitterly – and, as will be seen later, Guettard was a forerunner of both the contending parties.

Geology had not yet become a science. But it was on its way to attaining that status; already its students realized that the Earth was far older and had developed through a far more complicated process than had been supposed. Above all, they understood what technique progress demanded: first-hand study of the Earth itself.

Le Rocher-St-Michel at Le Puy in the Auvergne: this volcanic neck, 280 ft high, is crowned by an eleventh century church built on the site of a Roman temple.

EXPLORATION AND TRAVEL

Exploration, astronomy and health

Exploration had meanwhile continued in the face of grave difficulties. Although as early as 1522 Magellan had crossed the Pacific, comparatively little was known, even in the eighteenth century, about that ocean.

It was not only the vast extent of the seas that made exploration hazardous, nor the scurvy that ravaged the crews on such long voyages. There was also the difficulty in ascertaining a vessel's exact position.

Latitude was fairly easy to obtain, now that the sextant had been invented, by 'shooting the Sun', but to determine longitude was far more difficult. For this the local time, as shown by the Sun, had to be compared with the time at some centre such as Greenwich, whose longitude was known. No clocks were as yet sufficiently accurate, but the sky could be made to serve as a clock, by noting the moment, by local time, when the Moon obscured a certain star and comparing this with the time when it obscured the same star as recorded at Greenwich or some other pre-arranged centre.

First, however, the stars had to be charted and the Moon's movements predicted very accurately. It was for such a purpose that Greenwich Observatory had been built in 1676, and that its results were published in the *Nautical Almanac*. And, for the same purpose, the British Admiralty sent an expedition to Tahiti to observe a transit of Venus in 1769.

The officer to whom they entrusted the task was James Cook, distinguished both as a cartographer and for the efficiency with which he had recorded an eclipse of the sun.

The transit was duly observed; what was more, the voyage to Tahiti had been accomplished with an unprecedented absence of serious illness among the crew. Cook had shown how health may be preserved during even a long voyage, not so much by a better-balanced diet as by insistence on the highest standards of cleanliness.

To observe the transit of Venus had not, however, been the expedition's real purpose. James Cook had been sailing under sealed orders.

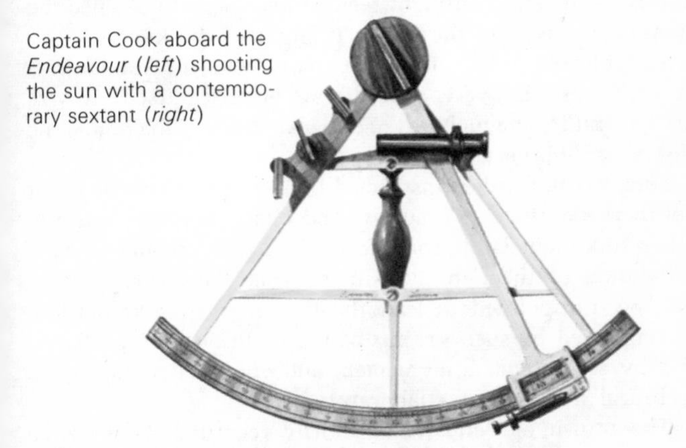

Captain Cook aboard the *Endeavour* (*left*) shooting the sun with a contemporary sextant (*right*)

Cook circumnavigated and charted New Zealand in 1769. Then he surveyed the east coast of Australia, running aground on the Great Barrier Reef (*opposite*). He sailed through the strait separating Australia from New Guinea and arrived back in England in July 1771.

Quest for the southern continent

Important discoveries had already been made in the Pacific; a number of islands and archipelagos had been found, and parts of the coasts of Australia, Tasmania, and New Zealand. Yet these regions had not been charted accurately, their extent was unknown, and they seemed insignificant compared to the vast continent then thought to exist somewhere in the south. This continent seemed necessary to balance the great land masses of the north; it might – who knows? – be as suitable for colonization or exploitation, and redound as much to its discoverer's credit, as America itself. It was known rather vaguely as *Terra Australis Incognita,* 'the Unknown Southern Land'.

Cook's sealed orders instructed him to 'search for the Great Southern Continent', to survey and chart its coasts and any other unknown lands that he might discover, and to take possession of them in the King's name. This was why he had been appointed to lead the first *scientific* exploration, accompanied by such savants as the naturalist Joseph Banks and by artists and draughtsmen, and equipped with a good technical library and a laboratory.

The transit of Venus satisfactorily recorded, Cook sailed

westwards to New Zealand and by circumnavigating both its islands he showed that it did not, as had seemed possible, form part of that southern continent. Pushing on still further westwards, he reached a great unknown landmass, far too vast to be an island, that he called New South Wales. He might have regarded this as part of the southern continent had he not found it was bounded on the south by the sea.

This land was full of surprises, including animals and native races hitherto unknown, and Cook foresaw that it was admirably suited for agriculture. It also held an unpleasant surprise for explorers, the Great Barrier Reef, on which their vessel ran aground and was holed. Extricated and repaired only with difficulty, she made her way homewards through the Torres Strait.

In 1772 Captain Cook, as he now was, resumed his search for the Great Southern Continent, twice crossing the Antarctic Circle – the first explorer ever to venture so far south. Though he discovered other Pacific islands, he showed that the unknown southern land was a myth. If any great land mass existed, as he thought possible, it would lie too near the South Pole and be too bleak and desolate ever to be inhabited.

Reconstructions of the woolly rhinoceros and mammoth (*above*) that were discovered in the eighteenth century by Pallas. The fur on their skin showed that they were living during the Great Ice Age, as well as during milder periods.

Mammoths and mountains

While the expedition led by Cook was observing the 1769 transit of Venus and exploring the South Seas, another was making similar investigations among the land masses of the north.

Annoyed at hearing comments on the cultural backwardness of Russia, the Empress Catherine the Great had ordered her scientists to visit Siberia not only to observe the transit but to make a systematic study of her whole domain.

Headed by the German naturalist Peter Simon Pallas, a

team of savants set out from St Petersburg in 1768, returning six years later with a wealth of information about conditions throughout the Russian Empire.

There had long been a trade in ivory obtained from Siberia, where the existence of many strange animal bones had been reported. Pallas discovered that scattered over the region beyond the Urals and between the Altai Mountains and the Arctic coasts, were countless elephant tusks and the bones of innumerable elephants, bison and rhinoceroses. Many of these creatures were of species now extinct – one is still known by the Russian name 'Mammoth' – and fur on patches of rhino skin showed that the local climate had once been temperate.

His researches in the Urals and the Altai convinced Pallas that mountain-chains are formed of three different types of rock. Their central core consists of a lofty mass of such hard materials as granite, some of which are bedded vertically or inclined steeply. Likewise sloping steeply along the sides of this central ridge, but flattening out away from them and becoming level on the plains, are lower mountains formed of beds of fossil-bearing limestone. Even further from the central core are foothills consisting of clays, marls, and sands.

Pallas believed that the central primitive rocks had once formed islands in a sea only about 650 feet deep that covered much of the earth. This sea had later deposited against its sides secondary limestone and tertiary mountains formed of softer rocks. Volcanoes, he thought, were due to the combustion of masses of iron pyrites derived from the primitive rocks, and it was their explosion that had raised such mountains as the Alps high above the sea.

Pallas stressed that previous theories of the Earth's structure had been based solely on the study of very limited regions and on the assumption that conditions were much the same all the world over. He, on the other hand, had made exhaustive observations covering a vast area which included some great mountain ranges. This had shown him the fallacy of supposing that the sea had ever risen high enough to cover the mountains; the caverns within the Earth, no matter how great or numerous they were, could never enable so vast a volume of water to flow away.

'I will lift up mine eyes unto the hills'

While Pallas was studying the structure of the Urals and the Altai, a Swiss naturalist named Horace Benedict de Saussure was investigating that of the Alps. He agreed with Pallas that their central core consists of granite, but he saw that in many places these so-called primitive rocks are intermingled with secondary limestones. He noticed too that in some of the mountains rock beds form great arches or troughs, or are even contorted into S-shaped folds, although their structure shows that they were originally deposited in horizontal layers on the sea floor. Unable to find any evidence of the action of subterranean fires, he could imagine no other cause for such great earth movements. Apart for a surmise that the rock beds had been contorted while they were still in a plastic condition, he offered no theory but said that he awaited the results of further observation.

De Saussure realized that mountain valleys could not, as some naturalists supposed, have been excavated by the sea; they must have been scooped out by water from melting mountain snows, by rain, or by rivers. He also explained that pebbles, whose origin had hitherto been something of a mystery, had likewise been transported to their present position by the action of running water and had become rounded and smoothed during the process.

Although he himself contributed little to geological theory, his years of work in the Alps provided a wealth of material for use by his successors, and he was the first to bring the words 'geology' and 'geologist' into general use.

De Saussure's enthusiasm for mountain scenery, which led him to the very summit of Mont Blanc, was so eloquently expressed in his descriptions of the Alps that it infected others and at last transformed the general outlook on mountains. Whereas mountains had hitherto been regarded with an almost superstitious dread, they were now found to be inspiring. Figuratively speaking, today's mountaineers, skiers, fell wenders, youth hostellers, hikers, and other votaries of high places are following the trail blazed by De Saussure, the first savant to glory in the name of geologist.

De Saussure's zeal over the Alps first popularized mountain climbing

THE NATURE AND FORMATION OF ROCK

The problem of basalt

When in 1752 a prize was offered for an essay on the possibility that Britain had once been joined to France, it was won by a brilliant young Frenchman, Nicholas Desmarest. Instead of merely theorizing, he pointed out, as Guettard had done, that the rocks on both sides of the English Channel are similar in structure; he added that Britain harbours noxious animals which nobody would have taken there and which certainly could not have swum across. Illustrating his contention with a chart, he inferred that the two countries had formerly been connected by an isthmus, across the Straits of Dover.

This achievement attracted influential attention, and in 1788 Desmarest became Inspector-General and Director of the Manufactures of France. Travelling widely in connection with his work, he grew interested in a perplexing problem.

What exactly was the dark stone called basalt, the stone whose strange columnar structure produced such spectacular scenery as the Giant's Causeway? A few suggestions had been made, but it hardly seemed plausible that the stone columns were immense crystals, or the petrified stems of a giant bamboo!

Guettard had suggested that basalt was aqueous in origin, but although it was in places interbedded with other rocks it showed no signs of a bedded structure. On the other hand, in some respects it resembled a lava flow, though it showed no traces of an eruptive origin, no volcanic cones or craters.

Desmarest knew of Guettard's discovery of the evidence of volcanic action in the Auvergne, and when he visited that region in 1765 he was astonished to find that some obvious lava streams ended in stone columns. This at once suggested basalt, but as usual he refrained from theorizing. He sent for pictures of the Giant's Causeway and specimens of the rock of which it was formed, and compared them with the scenery and lava flows of the Auvergne. Next year he began the task of making a careful study of the region, a study that was to last almost the rest of his life.

Basalt columns in the Auvergne

World-wide eruptive action?

Desmarest found the basaltic rocks in the Auvergne confusing. Some had the characteristic rough surface which showed that they were lava flows and were connected to the craters that had emitted them. Some were devoid of this rough surface, and could be seen on valley sides in positions that no streams of lava seemed likely to have reached. Some simply capped the tops of the hills.

After long investigation, he decided that many of the flows had once been rough but had been smoothed by the weather. Some of the more isolated masses of lava, he surmised, were the remains of former craters, but many of the basalt cappings on the hills had formed part of a lava flow until the intervening sections had been worn away by streams. Guettard and others had realized that river valleys had been formed by the water that flowed along them; Desmarest showed clearly, with examples, that this process had actually taken place.

There had, he at last inferred, been three distinct periods of volcanic activity in the Auvergne. The most recent had produced continuous streams of lava, their surface in some

The Giant's Causeway with inset showing detail of hexagonal columns

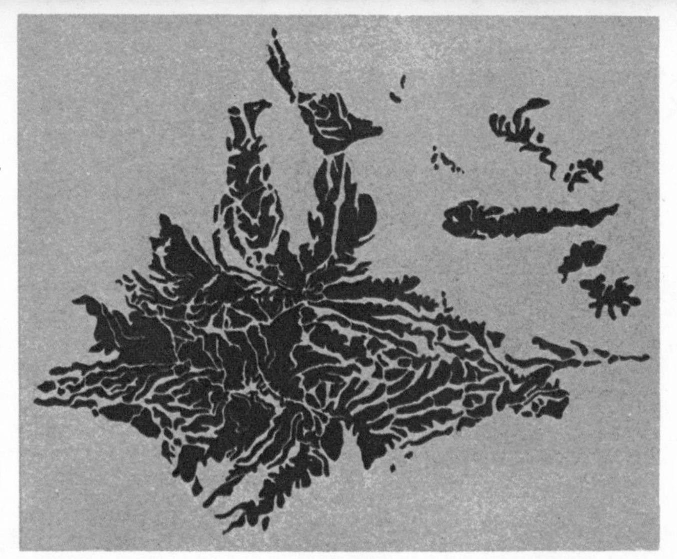

Part of Desmarest's map of the lava flows in the Auvergne

places worn smooth by the weather, and grooved but not cut right through by streams. Some of the lava had flowed into valleys which already existed when the eruption took place, and it now lined their sides.

During the second period, lava flows had poured out before such valleys were formed, and in these the rocks had been deeply trenched and carved into isolated masses of basalt by river action. The most ancient lava flows seemed to have been emitted by submarine volcanoes, for they lay beneath or were interbedded with ordinary sedimentary rocks.

Desmarest was a deliberate worker, and his detailed map of the Auvergne was not published during his lifetime. Had it appeared earlier it might have aroused some excitement, for his views were far more comprehensive than those of Guettard. The latter had announced evidence for the existence of former volcanoes in the heart of France, and that was surprising enough . But that a widespread rock like basalt should be of eruptive origin implied that much of western Europe had once been the scene of volcanic activity! Many thinkers found this idea difficult to believe, and soon it was contradicted in no uncertain voice.

Mineral identification

When, in 1775, a new instructor in mineralogy was needed at the Mining Academy of Freiberg in Saxony, the position was filled by Abraham Gottlob Werner. Then 26, Werner had studied the subject almost from the cradle. His first playthings had been pieces of rock, and his reward for diligence was to be shown his father's collection of minerals. While he was a student at the Academy he had toiled underground with the miners, and he had studied mining law at Leipzig University.

No better choice could have been made; in his hands what had been a mere technical school acquired almost university status. Not only was he lucid in his explanations, devoted to his students and ready to take any trouble on their behalf, but he was also a man of great charm and personal magnetism, with an amazing gift of imparting his own views and enthusiasms to others.

To Werner's mind, mineralogy was the key to the history

Based on a drawing by Jameson of the rocks in a Scottish cliff. As veins of granite-gneiss penetrate the other rocks, he regarded this as evidence favouring Werner's theory that the granite was formed like the other rocks as a hardened sludge on the sea floor.

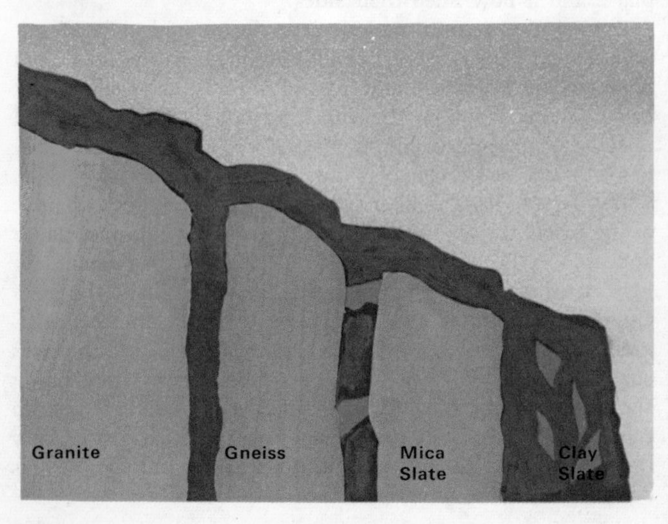

of the world. For, he reasoned, did not the minerals compose the rocks, and did not the rocks mould the Earth's physical features, and did not these features sway the fortunes of peace and war?

Shortly before his appointment, Werner had compiled a manual on the external characteristics of minerals. It classified minerals not by their composition, since the science of chemistry was not sufficiently far advanced at that time, but by such qualities as their feel, their hardness, coldness to the touch, brittleness and structure, as well as by their crystal form. Yet this was the first methodical treatment of the subject, and it was of the greatest help alike to the mining engineer and to the student of geology.

Not that Werner would have dreamed of using such a word, even had it then been in vogue. He called the study of rocks and their structure – which developed from the study of minerals – *geognesy* (knowledge of the Earth), defining this as practical first-hand investigation of the materials that constitute the terrestrial globe. He and his disciples were men who disdained the high-faluting notions of the cosmologists and of those who produced such 'monstrosities' as a so-called 'Theory of the Earth'.

Based on Werner's illustrations of crystal forms

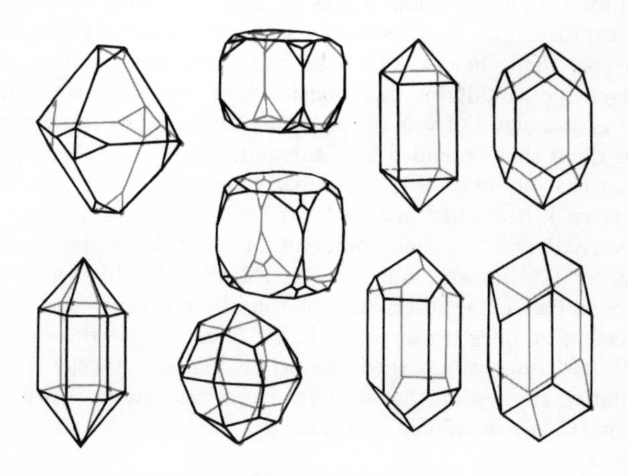

An all-embracing ocean?

True to his own ideals, Werner based his teaching on his first-hand investigations of the rocks of Saxony, which he assumed to be typical of those of the whole earth. Convinced from their structure that, except from some scattered superficial layers, these rocks had all been formed under water, he deduced that the Earth had long been covered by an ocean so deep that it submerged the very mountain tops, and he classified the rocks in the order and manner in which he thought they had been produced.

The oldest *primitive* rocks, he held, consisted of a hardened chemical sludge from the floor of that world-wide ocean. The most ancient rock of all was granite, and these rocks also included basalt.

Next came the *transitional* rocks, partly a hardened sludge from that sea floor and partly a hardened sediment. They included some limestones and the hard grey sandstones that the miners called *grauwacke*. More recent still were *floetz* or bedded rocks completely formed of hardened sediment and ranging from sandstone and limestone to rock salt and coal.

The superficial beds that occurred only in localized areas comprised such alluvial rocks as recently-formed clays, sands, gravels, and peats as well as volcanic rocks. The latter, he believed, were produced by combustion of coal seams.

As for the idea that basalt was an eruptive rock, he admitted that in some places it had a 'pseudo-volcanic' appearance, but explained this as being caused by fires in the coal fields below. When he had examined a hill in the Erzgebirge mountains that consisted of layers of sand and gravel and clay but was capped with basalt, he had observed that these rocks blended into one another. Here, he felt, was proof that, in spite of its columnar structure, basalt, like the other rock beds, had been formed beneath the sea.

Notwithstanding their contempt for 'Theories of the Earth', Werner's followers failed to notice that he himself was responsible for another, that of the all-embracing sea. The question at once arose, what had become of all this water that had once submerged the whole Earth? Except for a tentative suggestion that it might have been swept away by a comet, Werner failed to reply.

Based on a sketch of a hill in the Erzebirge drawn by Werner's biographer Richard Beck. The section shows that it consists of a sheet of basalt, decomposed at its base, resting on layers of sand and gravel. Werner regarded this as evidence that all these rocks, including the basalt, had been formed as sediment on the sea floor.

The Earth's internal heat

The *Transactions* for 1785 of the newly-formed Royal Society of Edinburgh included a paper by Dr James Hutton, a gentleman-farmer whose interest in the land had led him to study geology. His *Theory of the Earth* aroused much controversy for it flatly contradicted Werner's teachings.

Hutton realized, as Werner had done, that bedded rocks – limestones and standstones and so forth – are hardened sediments laid down upon the sea floor. Unlike Werner, however, he did not regard them all as comparatively recent. Their varying degrees of hardness indicated, he declared, that they differ widely in age. Some indeed he described as primitive, meaning not that they were the oldest of the Earth's rocks, but that they were the oldest so far discovered.

He could imagine only one force that could have hardened them so completely and raised them from a former sea floor to become dry land – for unlike Werner he believed not that the sea had disappeared but that the land had risen above it.

Impression, from an old engraving, of the Earth's internal heat

That force was the internal heat of the Earth – and it was this heat that produced volcanoes.

He may have been influenced by his friendship with James Watt, whose steam engine demonstrated the immense thrusting power which heat can generate. It was, moreover, this heat that had caused ordinary bedded rocks to be penetrated by veins of larger masses of very different types of rock. These, Hutton declared, had been formed by the cooling of molten material, and they ranged from the concretions in the clay-ironstone to granite itself.

This suggestion of the origin of granite was unprecedented; Werner had declared Scottish granite to be the very oldest primitive rock, formed as a hardened sludge from the sea floor. Not even Desmarest, who had surprised the scientific world by showing that basalt is of volcanic origin, had regarded granite as other than sedimentary. And here was James Hutton declaring that it had been produced not by water but by heat!

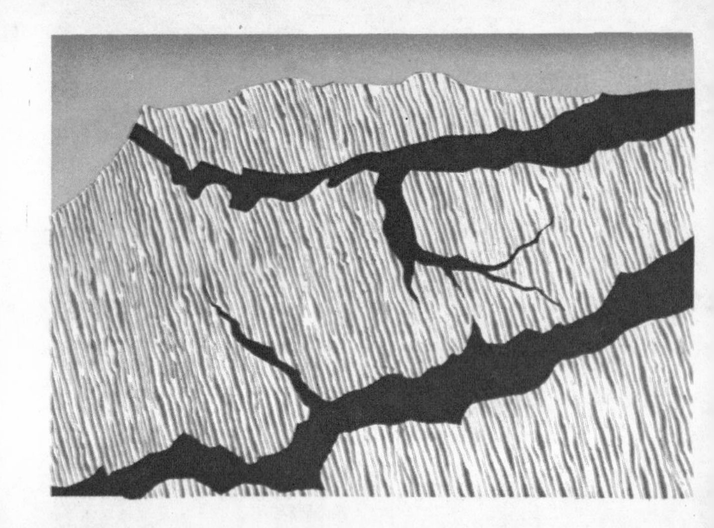

'No vestige of a beginning – no prospect of an end'

Hutton's startling theory was rendered even more unacceptable by the forbidding clumsiness of his literary style. Even its title was unfortunate. *Theory of the Earth* suggested another cosmogony, another attempt to explain the Earth's origin on general lines.

This work, therefore, attracted little attention until, in 1793, it was denounced by a Wernerian mineralogist, not so much on technical as on theological grounds. Hutton was accused of holding 'atheistic opinions'. He had, it was alleged, contradicted both *Genesis* and the *Book of Revelation* by declaring that the Earth had had, and would have, neither beginning nor end!

Hutton was distressed at this attack on him, for he was a deist and a sincerely religious man. He then expounded his views at still greater length in his book *Theory of the Earth, with Proofs and Illustrations* in 1795.

This was no more attractively written than the first book had been and it was almost disregarded until after Hutton's death. Then his friend John Playfair, expounded the theme of the book in a much more lucid work, *Illustrations of the Huttonian Theory of the Earth* (1802).

Illustrating Hutton's theory, these diagrams show veins of granite traversing schist

One illustration of the theory elucidated unconformities within the rocks, where one series of rock beds lies almost horizontally upon the upturned edges of another. It explained that although the lower rock beds had been deposited horizontally on the sea floor, they must have been bodily twisted and raised to reach their present position. Then they had been lowered to become another sea floor on which accumulated the sediment later hardened to form the upper rock beds. Elsewhere, too, rock beds originally deposited horizontally had been crumpled into folds. Here again such effects could have been produced only by one force, the Earth's internal heat.

Similar processes were still going on for, as Hutton explained, the Earth's surface was being steadily washed away by the rivers and the rain; what was more, they seemed likely to continue. It was in this sense, and in this sense only, that Hutton had ended his theory with the words that had been so badly misunderstood:

'It results, therefore, from our present enquiry, that we find no vestige of a beginning – no prospect of an end'.

Based on a section from d'Aubuisson's *Traité de Géognosie* across England from Wales to London. Dip of rocks greatly exaggerated.

Werner's crowning achievement

One of Werner's students, the young Frenchman Jean d'Aubuisson, accepted his theory of the origin of the basalt of Saxony but doubted whether it applied elsewhere. Advised to study conditions in the Auvergne, he decided that the rocks could not possibly be of volcanic origin, for Werner had taught that eruptions are always caused by the combustion of subterranean coal, and here the basalt lay on a thick bed of granite!

When, however, he saw what were obviously the craters of extinct volcanoes and traced the streams of lava which they had emitted, his opinion changed and in 1819 he announced that *all* basalt is of volcanic origin.

A German student, Leopold von Buch, similarly accepted Werner's basalt theory, and he too visited the Auvergne. In the Puy de Dôme region he studied a number of strangely-shaped hills towering above a granite plateau. These *puys*, he declared, consisted of granite plugs forced upwards and

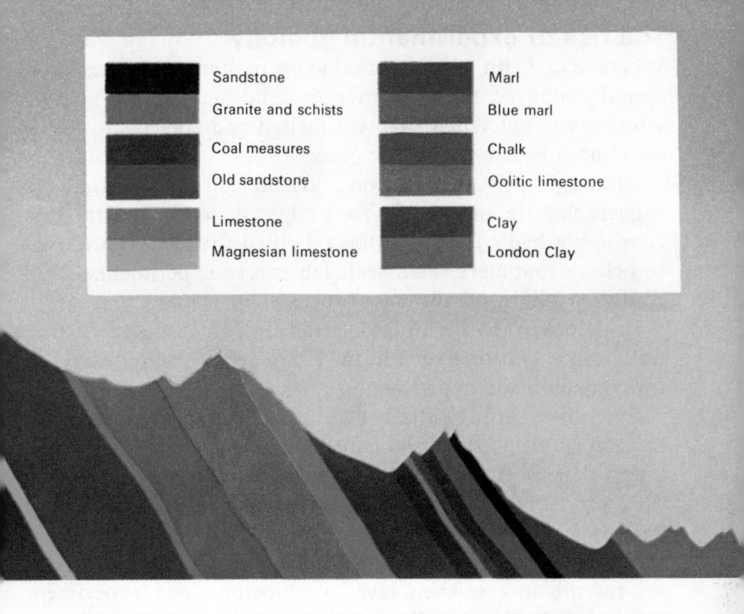

transformed into a rock, which he called domite, by immense volumes of water or acid vapour from underground. If a bubble of this vapour burst at their top it produced a crater, but otherwise the puys were left with a rounded summit. For a time he still felt, however, that the basalt of Germany might be a hardened chemical sludge.

His visits to Scandinavia and to the volcanic islands of the Atlantic revolutionized his views, and he rejected Werner's belief that the mountains of central Europe had been completely covered by the sea. Instead he held that they had been raised by earth movements, and it was on this theory that he based his geological map of Germany (1824), the first to cover so large an area.

Though neither d'Aubuisson nor von Buch formally renounced Wernerian views, they increasingly adopted those of Hutton. Whatever faults there were in his geognosy, Werner had none the less helped to lay the foundations of mineralogical science, and his crowning achievement consisted in the brilliant geologists, including d'Aubuisson and von Buch, whom he had inspired and trained.

The rise of experimental geology

When in a Leith glass works some molten glass was accidentally allowed to cool slowly it solidified into an opaque white mass, but when this was melted and cooled quickly it once more became ordinary glass.

Although this led Hutton's friend, Sir James Hall, to suggest that the nature of a rock might depend upon the rate at which it had cooled, Hutton ridiculed the idea. He refused to believe that mere small-scale laboratory experiments could throw any light on the vast processes of Nature.

In deference to his opinion, Hall did not proceed further until after Hutton's death in 1797, when he felt free to proceed with his experiments.

Extending through the bedded rocks round Edinburgh are thin layers of a basalt-like substance called whinstone. Hall found that when fragments of this rock were cooled quickly they produced a sort of glass, but when this was remelted and cooled very slowly it again resembled whinstone.

While visiting the Italian volcanoes he was impressed with the resemblance of their lava to whinstone, and experiment showed that when melted and cooled at different rates it behaved exactly as that rock did. Some sheets of hardened lava are vertical, and Hall realized that the molten material in these had been forced upwards from within the Earth, and that the 'dykes' of vertical sheets of whinstone in the Scottish rocks had been similarly formed.

Limestone, when heated strongly, gives off carbon dioxide and becomes quicklime. When it is intensely heated in sealed iron tubes, Hall found that it is transformed into a material resembling marble; and by heating a layer of sand at the bottom of a cauldron filled with brine he converted it into sandstone.

By placing a number of layers of clay or cloth under heavy pressure and then compressing them laterally he forced them into folds closely resembling the contortions in the rock layers that form the Berwickshire cliffs.

Thus Hall's experiments show that laboratory work can throw light on the vast processes of Nature. They indeed confirmed Hutton's theory that many of the Earth's rocks have been produced not by water action but by intense heat.

Foldings in the rocks of the Berwickshire cliffs (*top*) compared with those produced by Sir James Hall in the laboratory by compressing layers of clay or cloth.

Neptunists and Vulcanists

In the 1800s Edinburgh became a centre for geological enquiry – and for geological controversy. It was here, where Hutton had published his *Theory of the Earth*, that his *Theory* was being denounced as a 'monstrosity'.

Robert Jameson, Professor of Natural History at Edinburgh University, had spent two years studying geognosy under Werner, who had imbued him not only with his own enthusiasm for that subject but with his power of imparting it to others. In 1808 he founded the Wernerian Natural History Society of Edinburgh, whose purpose seemed to be to interpret the geology of Scotland along lines worked out in the coal-measures of Saxony.

The dispute about the nature of basalt flared up again, and Scottish beauty spots were enlivened by argumentative groups of geognosists and geologists. The former were eager to show that the layers of whinstone had begun as a chemical sludge among the bedded rocks, while the latter were equally anxious to prove that it had been forced into their midst as a molten magma by heat and pressure from below.

Arthur's Seat, Edinburgh, the remains of an extinct volcano

The academic calm of Edinburgh was likewise enlivened, for the discussions between the two factions were apt to get acrimonious. Jameson, who denied any evidence of volcanic action in Scotland, sneered at those 'fire-philosophers', the *Vulcanists*. They, who because of their belief in the Earth's central heat were also called *Plutonists*, naturally retaliated by chaffing the geognosists who believed in Werner's all-embracing ocean as *Neptunists*.

A fair-minded man and a true scientist, Jameson would never have dreamed of suppressing or censoring a technical paper merely because he did not agree with it. During the thirty years covered by the *Memoirs* of the Wernerian Society, the tone of its contents gradually changed from Neptunism to something not far removed from Vulcanism.

The dispute between Neptunists and Vulcanists petered out, but it had meantime focussed attention upon the evidence that rocks gave on the Earth's history. It had ignored any evidence they might be given regarding the former inhabitants of the Earth.

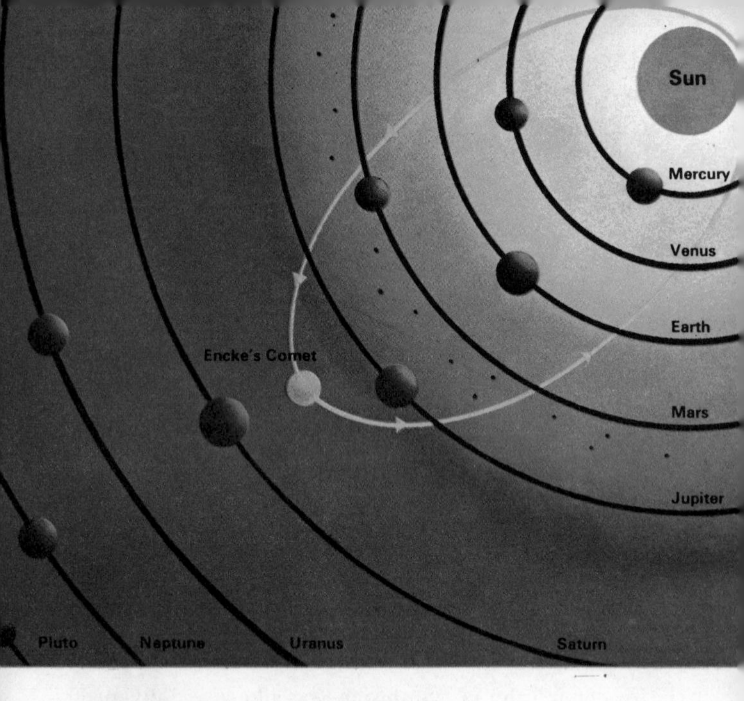

ADVANCES IN ASTRONOMY

'Other worlds than ours'

Astonishing advances were now being made in astronomy. Two new planets, as well as a score or so of satellites, were discovered: Uranus by Herschel in 1781 and Neptune by La Verrier and Adams in 1785. A third outer planet, Pluto, was not discovered by Tombaugh until 1930.

These discoveries harmonized with the 'nebular hypothesis' put forward in 1798 by Laplace. On this theory the Solar System had originated from jets of incandescent gas thrown off from the swiftly rotating Sun by centrifugal force. After similarly throwing off smaller spurts of gas which formed the satellites, these jets had become the planets. Such discoveries did not deny the fascinating speculation that the Planets, and possibly some of the other heavenly bodies, might be inhabited. It had been raised as early as 1686 by Fontenelle and was revived about 1860 by the astronomer Flammarion.

It seemed justified when, in 1877, Schiaparelli announced

that he had seen 'channels' on Mars – especially as the Italian word he used, *canali*, was misread as meaning artificial waterways! The obvious deduction was that Mars was inhabited by intelligent beings and as, according to the nebular hypothesis, that planet had been thrown off from the Sun ages before the Earth, the further implication was that the Martian race was more ancient, and more 'advanced' than mankind.

Another nineteenth-century discovery suggested, on mathematical grounds, that an unknown planet might exist between Mars and Jupiter; there proved, however, to be not one planet but several hundred planetoids, the asteroids. The theory that these might have been formed by a disrupted planet was put forward by Olbers, who had discovered the second of them in 1802, and this idea is now returning to favour. One suggestion is that the explosion was caused by the impact upon a sizeable planet of a much smaller body like an immense meteor. There is no general agreement on this, however, and it is held that further research is needed.

The Solar System with the orbit of Enck's Comet (*left*). View of Mars showing 'canals' (*below*)

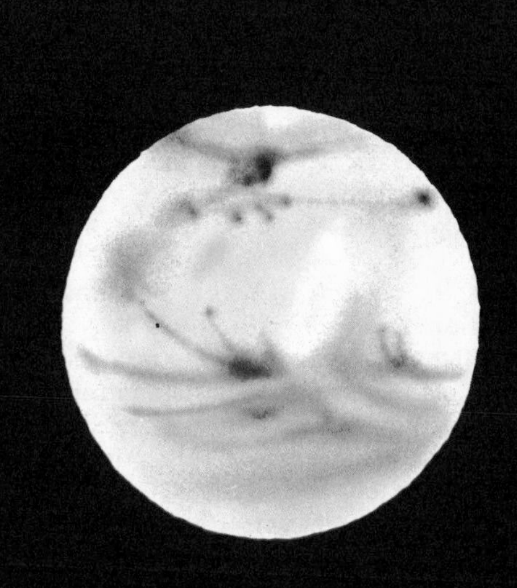

The Galaxy seen from space indicating position of the Solar System

A lifeless Universe?

Herschel had discovered Uranus while making a systematic study of the sky, and this had led to other discoveries which were even more unexpected. Since the time of Copernicus it had been held that the Sun, and not the Earth, is at the centre of the Universe. Herschel showed that the Sun is in fact nowhere near the centre – and, what was more, that it is actually moving among the stars, taking the Solar System with it.

These stars, it now appeared, are really Suns, and millions of them constitute our Galaxy, the Milky Way. The Galaxy is shaped like a flattened disc with two spiral arms, all consisting of stars. Many of these stars form clusters and other groupings, and Herschel's study of double stars showed that Newton's Law of Gravitation is no mere local ruling; it prevails not only within, but beyond, our Solar System.

Nebulas, patches of light among the stars, perplexed him. Some consisted of myriads of stars, others of clouds of misty light. The former, Herschel surmised, might be beyond the Galaxy, and they are now known to be other galaxies far distant from our own.

There are indeed millions of these 'island universes', some spiral like the Milky Way, some oval, and some irregular in shape. Each consists of innumerable stars; and as, according to the nebular hypothesis, each star might well have its own family of planets, the number of inhabited worlds might be very large indeed.

But sentimental beliefs in 'other worlds than ours' were then shattered. Improved telescopes showed that the alleged canals of Mars were optical illusions, and the nebula hypothesis was abandoned as untenable. The 'tidal hypothesis' that superseded it implied that planets were formed only when one star passed so close to another as to rip fragments from its edge.

As such near-collisions seemed likely to be rare, only a small minority of the stars seemed likely to have planets. There was even the possibility that throughout all Creation our Earth might be the only place where life could exist.

Nebula

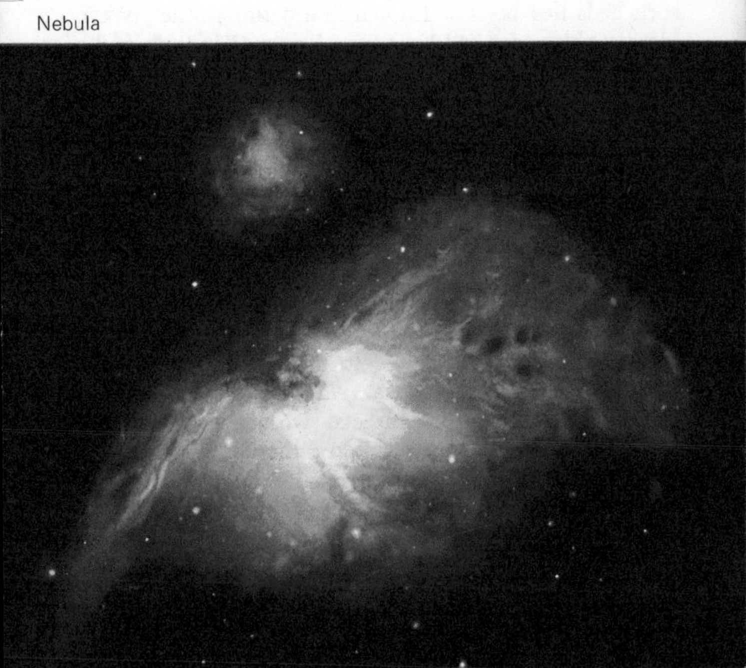

STRATIGRAPHICAL GEOLOGY AND PALAEONTOLOGY

Rock beds of France

Though Neptunists and Vulcanists agreed that the different rock beds had been laid down in a definite order, Werner's ideas of this order had been mistaken and Hutton's had been vague. A method of ascertaining the geological succession was however found independently of both schools of thought.

Kinds of fossils obviously vary from rock to rock and from place to place, and about 1780 the Abbé Giraud-Soulavie used their differences as a means of estimating the chronological sequence of the beds of limestones in the mountains of southern France. His work received little attention, and it was some time before this method was used in a region which had attracted geologists from Guettard onwards.

The Chevalier de Lamarck had made his name as a botanist, but when he was appointed to the Jardin des Plantes, the Paris *Museum d'Histoire Naturelle*, it was as professor of a branch of zoology, 'of insects, worms, and microscopic animals'. This led him to study the fossils of the Paris Basin and to produce a seven-volume treatise (1815–22) on 'Animals without Backbones'. He might be regarded as the founder of *invertebrate* palaeontology.

His smaller work *Hydrogéologie* was an enquiry into the effects not only of water itself but of living creatures upon the Earth's crust. Lamarck realized and indeed exaggerated the destructive effects of flowing water and of weathering; he believed that the ground had originally been level, and that mountains were all that were left when other rocks had been eroded away. While conceding the possibility of local earth movements and volcanic action affecting the Earth's crust, he did not believe in former far-reaching floods or other world-wide catastrophies.

On somewhat similar lines, Lamarck held that the ocean beds had been scooped out partly by the scouring action of the tides and partly by a slow westward movement of the waters, caused chiefly by the Moon. This slowly destroyed the eastern shores of the land masses, while their area was meantime being extended westwards by the deposition of sediment brought down by the rivers. In this process earth movements had no share; the continents were driven passively around the world.

Fossiliferous limestone (*opposite*) and its included shells from the Paris region

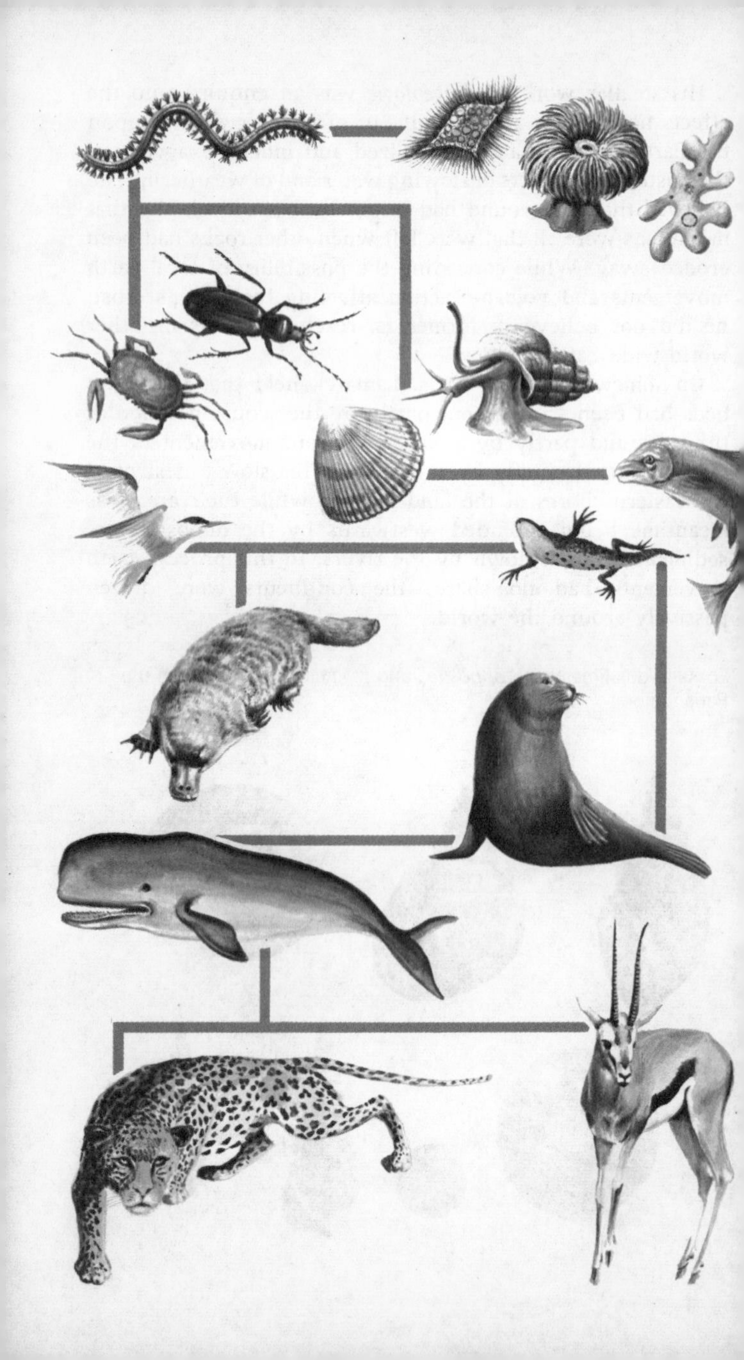

Inheritance of acquired characters?

Lamarck's sole evidence for this theory lay in fossils, which were a conclusive proof that the sea had once flowed over what is now dry land. He was the first to restrict this term to its present meaning. Hitherto it had signified anything dug out of the ground, but now it replaced the older term 'figured stones', for Lamarck defined fossils as 'the still recognizable remains of organized bodies'.

It was these organized bodies, he believed, that had formed the Earth's crust. All compound bodies, he pointed out, tend to decay into their components, and the only thing that could recombine them was the 'life force'. Some masses of limestone are obviously coral reefs, and coal is petrified wood – and now on the same lines all rocks 'without exception' were declared to be a by-product of life!

Werner had taught that granite was a hardened sludge from the depths of an all-embracing ocean, and Hutton that it had cooled and solidified from a molten magma – and now Lamarck averred that it had been produced from the remains of dead plants and animals accumulated on the sea floor!

He had noticed that the more recent the rock beds, the more complex and 'advanced' are the fossils they contain, and he felt that it was impossible to believe that all the countless species of living creatures had been separately created. This led him to frame a theory of *Transformism*, or Evolution as it is now called.

Lamarck believed not only that all plants and animals were ultimately descended, over long eras, from simpler forms of life, but that their development had been due to the 'inheritance of acquired characters'. The structure of some creature's body might undergo a slight change either through the effects upon it of its surroundings or through its own efforts to cope with them. This change might be passed on to its offspring, and the slow piling-up over the ages of a succession of such changes might in the long run cause its distant descendants to be completely transformed. To illustrate his theory he drew up a 'genealogical tree', showing how the different types of animal life might be related.

Illustration of Lamarck's idea of a genealogical tree

Fossil skeleton of a *Plesiosaurus* discovered at Lyme Regis during Cuvier's researches on fossil bones

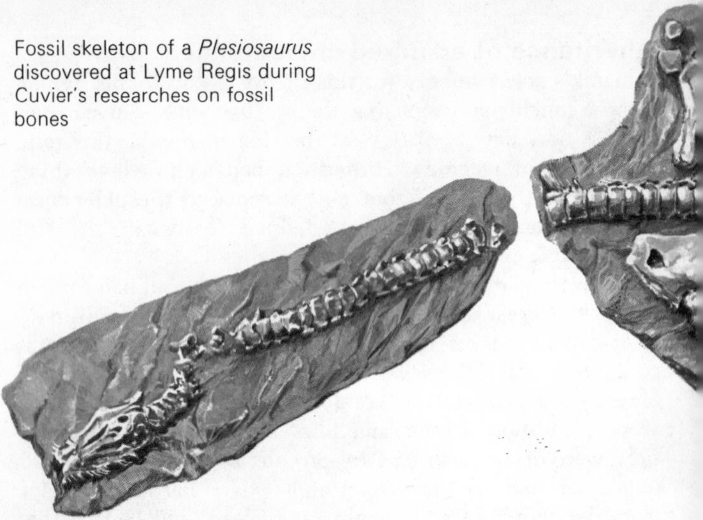

Succession of catastrophes?

The fossils of the Paris Basin had inspired Lamarck with his theory of evolution; they made another biologist reject all such theories completely. When examining these fossils the zoologist Cuvier decided to compare them with modern living creatures of similar types. After studying a number of skeletons, he showed that the elephants whose remains had been unearthed belonged to an entirely different species from that of the two varieties of modern elephant. Through his demonstration that some fossils are those of creatures quite unlike any of those of today, that indeed some of these animals are now completely extinct, he has been acclaimed as the founder of *vertebrate* palaeontology.

Somewhat hampered in his work by his lack of geological experience, he joined forces with a leading mineralogist, Alexandre Brongniart. Together they spent years studying the geology of the Seine valley; after tracing and mapping its strata, they showed (1811) that each of these is differentiated by its own characteristic fossils, and they were impressed by the regular sequence of rock beds occurring over a distance of about 75 miles.

Following up their work, Omalius d'Halloy obtained similar

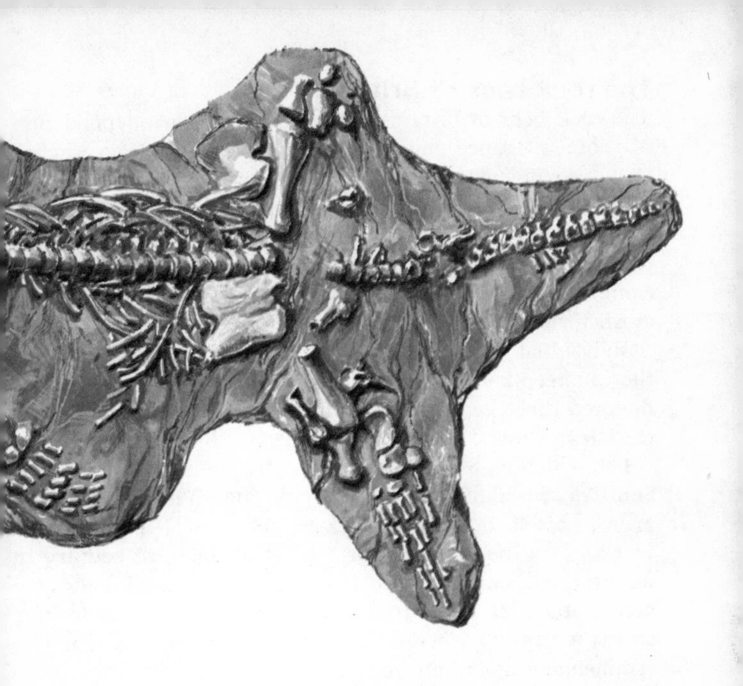

results over a wider area and in more ancient strata. This enabled him to construct a geological map of a broad area of France that was far more explanatory than Guettard's pioneer effort.

Cuvier realized, as clearly as did Lamarck, that the older a rock bed is, the simpler and less 'advanced' are the fossils it contains. Unlike Lamarck, however, he completely rejected all transformist (evolutionary) theories; such ideas, he felt, were contradicted by the complete lack of any evidence that creatures intermediate between two biological species had ever existed.

He believed, on the other hand, that the Earth had undergone a succession of such catastrophies as overwhelming floods which had destroyed all its inhabitants, the most recent having occurred about five or six thousand years ago. After each of these disasters, he declared, the world had been re-peopled by a new creation of plants and animals differing in certain respects from their forerunners.

The rock beds of Britain

The rock beds of Britain were studied almost independently of those in France, and in 1760 the Reverend John Michell found an ingenious way of illustrating their sequence. If a number of sheets of paper of various colours were pasted together and bent up along the middle to form a ridge, and if this were planed level and its middle again slightly lifted, it would, he explained, form 'a good general representation of most, if not all, large tracts of mountain scenery'.

Individual areas were also investigated in detail. Early in the nineteenth century the artist-geologist Thomas Webster devoted three years to the study of the coasts of Dorset and the Isle of Wight, publishing in 1815 an album of the scenery.

Far wider was the area covered by the work of William Smith, a self-educated land surveyor and civil engineer, who even in his schooldays was a keen collector of fossils. While working on the levellings of a canal in the west country in about 1793, Smith realized that although the rock beds may seem quite flat, they really slope gently downwards 'like so many slices of bread and butter', and he felt that this arrangement must be significant.

Study of rocks further afield confirmed his suspicion that 'each stratum contained organized fossils peculiar to itself and might . . . be recognized and discriminated from others like it . . . by examination of them'.

Interest in geology was now widespread, and in 1799 William Smith was able to astonish two clergymen by telling them more about the fossils in their collection than they knew themselves, and he also pointed out something which they had not noticed, that a stratum of rock may be identified by its fossils. Preparing from his dictation a list of every geological formation from coal to chalk, with notes on the type of scenery which it produced and on its characteristic fossils, they circulated it among some of the leading geologists in Europe. Had his list been published in Britain, 'Strata Smith', as he was called, would at once have been recognized as one of the world's foremost geologists.

A view of part of the coast of the Isle of Wight that was studied and illustrated by the artist-geologist Thomas Webster

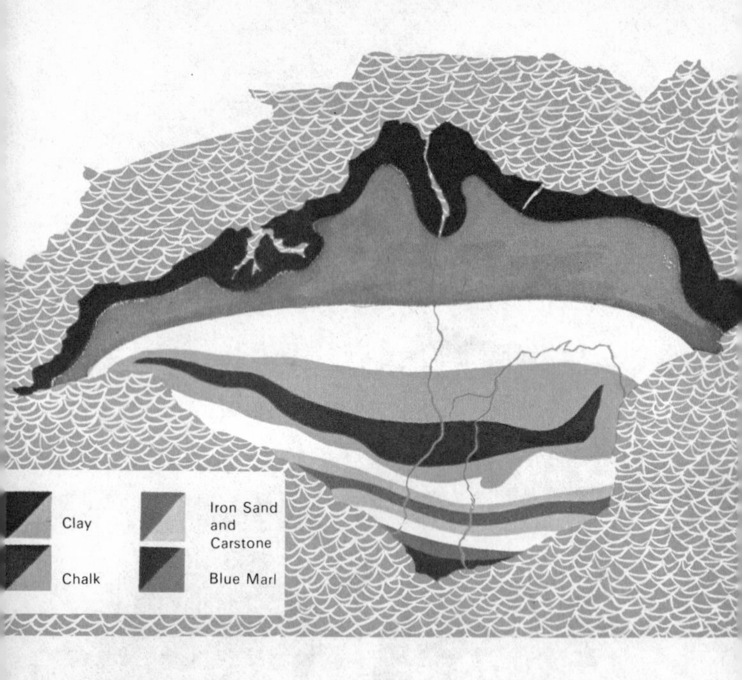

The first geological map of England

William Smith had, however, a far more ambitious project in mind, that of producing a geological map of England, Wales, and part of Scotland. Devoting over twenty years to its preparation and preceding it by a specimen county map of Somerset, he then had great difficulty in finding a publisher, and it was not until 1815 that his map appeared.

On a scale of five miles to the inch, it used a score of hues to distinguish the different formations, and brought out their sequence more clearly by darkening the colour of their bases. It was accompanied by a *Memoir* which displayed illustrative sections, and this introduced into geological literature terms taken from the rustic names used for some of the rock beds: Cornbrash, Clunch Clay, Forest Marble, and Lias ('Layers').

The value of this map is shown by the praise that d'Aubuisson gave it: 'what the most distinguished mineralogists had done over half a century for a little part of Germany, had been

The map (*opposite*) is based on William Smith's representation of the Isle of Wight on his geological map of England and Wales. The 'Iron Sand and Carstone' is now known as 'Lower Greensand' and 'Blue Marl' as 'Gault Clay'. (*Right*) fossil of a ganoid fish similar to those found in Scotland by Hugh Miller (see page 95)

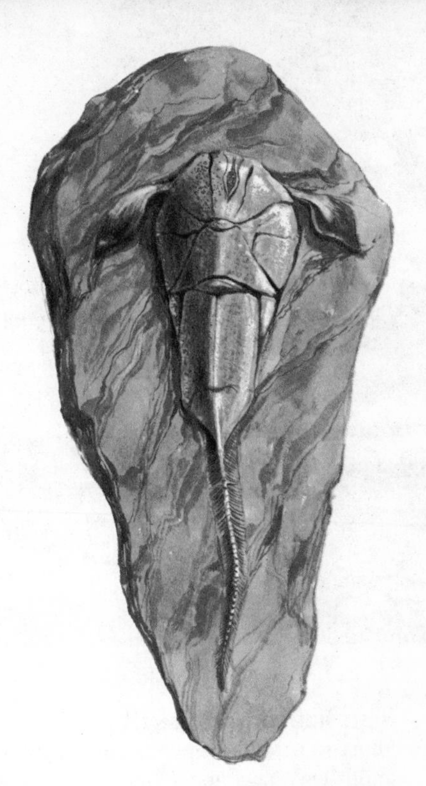

undertaken and accomplished for the whole of England by one man'.

Smith followed up this achievement by some geological maps of individual counties and by several works on fossils. In one of the latter he tried to make his representations of fossils look more natural by illustrating each on paper of a colour resembling that of the rock from which it came.

Aware that 'the theory of geology was in the possession of one class of man, the practise in another', he certainly did much to reconcile the two aspects of the science. He was brought almost to the verge of ruin but toiled on and at last he received the recognition his services to the country deserved. He was awarded a small pension from the Crown and was honoured by the recently-formed Geological Society, whose President hailed him as 'the father of English geology'.

Fish lizard and fossil fish

Shortly after the opening of the nineteenth century a small child was taking to her father one of the queer-looking objects that visitors to Lyme Regis liked to buy. Then a lady offered her half-a-crown for it! This naturally made little Mary Anning hunt for fossils in real earnest, and she was so successful that she made a living selling them. Not content with this, she studied them and became able to discuss them so knowledgeably that she gained a reputation as a palaeontologist. The local rocks, which consist of alternate beds of shale and limestone are exceptionally rich in fossils of creatures that lived in the age of reptiles and, as the shore was being incessantly worn away by the tide, there were always new specimens for Mary to discover.

Her more spectacular finds included the first complete skeleton of a plesiosaurus and the first specimen of a pteranadon found in Britain. Another discovery made in 1810, when she was only eleven years old, was thought worthy of mention in a collection of edifying verses intended for the young:

'Miss Anning as a child
ne'er passed
A pin upon the ground,
But picked it up, and so at
last
An ichthyosaurus found.'

In 1820, a young Scotsman, who had refused to attend University because none of the professions attracted him, started work as a quarryman, and found that the rocks abounded in fossils. Thus Hugh Miller found his twofold vocation, as an author and as a geologist. His best-known book, *The Old Red Sandstone,* is both a work of literature and an excellent guide to the fossils of Scotland, with special reference to the extinct ganoid fish. It moreover displays a deep religious sense, which led its author to entitle one of his later books *Footprints of the Creator*.

Geology in Britain owes much to such workers as William Smith and Mary Anning and Hugh Miller. Unmindful of, and caring nothing for, the rival theories of the Neptunists and Vulcanists, they simply studied the rocks and the fossils that they contained.

The Blue Lias rocks of Lyme Regis are rich in Mesozoic fossils, and it was on the shore at their base that Mary Anning then a child of eleven, discovered the skeleton of an *Ichthyosaurus*.
(*Below*) the skeleton of an *Ichthyosaurus*, discovered by Mary Anning.

British geologists co-operate

As interest in geology spread, associations, mostly rather small and short-lived, were formed to promote its study. Feeling that something more systematic was needed, in 1807 'thirteen gentlemen' of London founded the Geological Society 'to investigate the mineral structure of the Earth'.

Though at the outset it might almost have been mistaken for a dining club of amateur geologists, the new society took its work seriously. As its numbers increased it became a centre for geological research and discussion; in 1825 it received its charter of incorporation and was numbered among the learned societies of Britain.

'Neither Vulcanists nor Neptunists nor Wernerians nor Huttonians', the Fellows of the Geological Society were 'plain men who felt the importance of a subject about which they knew very little'. Their views, however, became increasingly Huttonian, and it may have been this controversy that made them pay less attention to fossils than to

Based on an illustration in De La Beche's *How to Observe in Geology*: these two pictures represent a headland in which seen from one direction the rock beds appear perfectly level, whereas they really dip steeply.

minerals and to local geological structure. William Smith's achievement transformed their outlook and made them for a time concentrate on palaeontology to the detriment of other branches of the science.

The Society's *Transactions* first appeared in 1811, and some of its members also produced the handbooks and instructions for field workers that the increased popularity of the science now demanded. Notable among these were *Outlines of the Geology of England and Wales* by Conybeare and Phillips (1822) and *How to Observe in Geology* by H. T. De la Beche (1835).

The Geological Society could not cover the whole field, and other organizations appeared to cater for amateurs and students. Foremost among these is the Geologists' Association, founded in 1858 to foster the progress and diffusion of the science; among its activities are its practical field meetings in regions of special interest.

The Field Studies Council was formed in 1943 to obviate the possibility that the study of natural history should be a matter only of laboratory work and textbooks. In its field study centres such subjects as geology could be studied from the Earth itself.

GEOLOGY BECOMES A SCIENCE

'By causes now in operation'

A young Oxford student who had read a work on geology found the subject so interesting that he attended a course of lectures. They were given by Dr Buckland, a clergyman who believed, like Cuvier, that the science confirmed the Biblical accounts of Creation and the Flood.

Buckland's enthusiasm inspired his student, Charles Lyell, to devote his life to geology. Lyell travelled in Britain and abroad, consulted other geologists and read widely, Playfair's *Illustrations of the Huttonian Theory* impressing him deeply. His work in the field made him reject Buckland's views, and he decided to set out his own conclusions at length.

Most geological works hitherto written had been intended for scientists or technicians. What Lyell had in mind was a book for the public – not a mere 'popularization' but a comprehensive guide to the whole science. This task was more difficult than might be thought. It was, he found, easier to write for the scientific world than the general reader.

He foresaw that his book might lead to a dispute more bitter, because of its religious implications, than that between the Neptunists and the Vulcanists. Undeterred, he challenged 'catastrophic' ideas in the book's very title: *Principles of Geology, Being an Attempt to Explain the Former Changes of the Earth's Surface, by Reference to Causes Now in Operation.*

The book was as comprehensive as its title. It was indeed encyclopaedic in scope, and it appeared in several volumes, the first being published in 1830. Later he produced two shorter – but still bulky – works, *The Elements of Geology* (1838) and *The Students' Elements of Geology* (1871).

Lyell believed that 'the causes now in operation', such as weathering, the action of the sea and rivers – he later included that of the ice – volcanoes, and slow earth movements, were in fact sufficient to explain the Earth's geological history. This theory, the reverse of Buckland's 'catastrophism', became known rather clumsily as 'uniformitarianism'.

View of the Temple of Serapis near Naples showing evidence of earth movements, such as those which occurred recently

Part of the escarpment that produces the tremendous Niagara Falls

'He teaches us to understand them'

No sooner had Volume One of the *Principles* appeared than the discussions began. Lyell replied to the technical queries in the later volumes and in the book's many revisions.

A younger geologist commented, 'We collect the facts and Lyell teaches us to understand them.' This was only a half-truth, however. Lyell not only discussed the facts that other geologists had collected; he collected many of them himself. He travelled far afield in Europe and America, and where possible he based his writings on first-hand observation.

He also systematized the study of more recent rock beds, which the former geologists had tended to neglect, and classified them by the proportion of extinct species of shell-fish remains found in them compared with modern species.

The disputes which Lyell's books aroused were partly technical, partly theological. The 'catastrophists' thought that the successive disasters they believed in – a destruction of life on earth followed by a new creation – were due to the

direct intervention of the Almighty, and they felt it rather shocking to think that the Earth had developed with no such Divine acts of interposition. To the 'uniformitarians' the Divine power did not need to be displayed in dramatic acts of intervention. It was manifest throughout the whole of the Earth's development.

Thus the older catastrophic views were superseded by uniformitarianism. Like Lyell himself, the geologists still 'attempt to explain the former changes of the Earth's surface by the causes now in operation,' though these are known to be more numerous and more varied than he could have possibly foreseen. And among the results of his work 'Noah's Flood' came to be regarded not as a world-wide inundation but as a great, but more localized disaster.

Lyell has well been called 'the father of modern geology'. Thanks largely to his clear exposition of the results obtained by such investigators as himself, the subject had ceased to be a lore or a collection of facts used as a basis for highly-debatable theories. Geology had at last become a science.

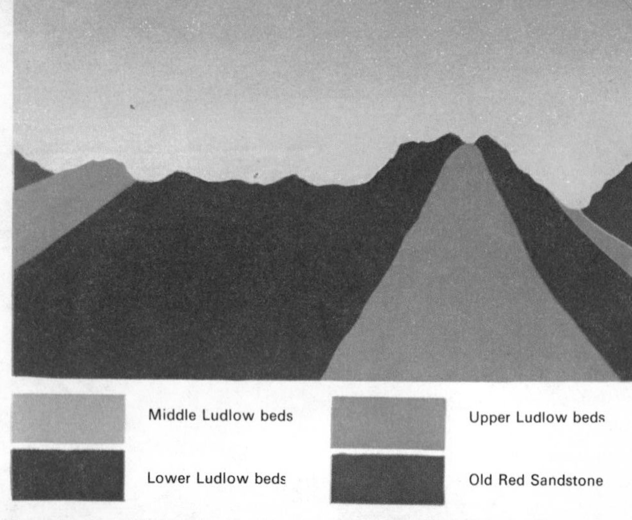

Based on an illustration in Murchison's *Siluria*, a fold in the rocks where the Silurian Ludlow beds underly the Old Red Sandstone

'The interminable greywacke'

The geology of much of the southeast of England was easy to understand. From the chalk down to the Old Red Sandstone, the rocks formed parallel layers dipping gently towards the southeast.

What lay beneath the Old Red Sandstone was far from clear. The rocks of most of Wales were by no means in orderly layers, 'like slices of bread and butter'. They were broken and crumpled, poor in fossils and extremely hard; Werner would have classed them as 'Grauwacke' or 'Transitional'. Some work had been done on them and some fossils collected, but they were not systematically investigated until 1831, when two geologists began to study them thoroughly.

Roderick Impey Murchison had been led to geology by Humphry Davy and trained in field work by Buckland. After six years' experience in other regions he decided to try to find some order in what he called the 'interminable greywacke' of Wales.

Realizing that he would have to begin where its rocks were in contact with those already known, he was directed by Buckland to the River Wye. He saw on the river bank some

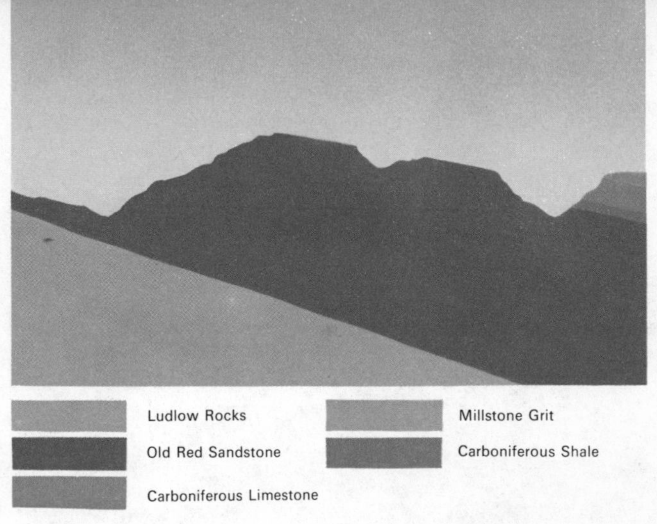

Based on an illustration showing the Old Red Sandstone underlying the rocks of the Carboniferous system, and with the Ludlow Rocks, the upper formation of the Silurian system, underlying the Old Red Sandstone

'low terrace-shaped ridges of grey rock, dipping slightly to the south-east and seeming to rise from beneath and to be parallel to the Old Red Sandstone of Herefordshire'. On crossing the river he was delighted to find that this rock teemed with transitional fossils!

'I had' he exulted 'got the upper grauwacke, so called, into my hands.' Tracing it far across country, he found that everywhere it rose from below the lowest beds of the Old Red Sandstone, and that all its strata were characterized by their own special fossils – a 'new step in British geology'. Using the methods of William Smith, he showed that these were applicable to rocks Smith never saw, and that there seemed no reason why they should not be applicable everywhere.

He knew that 'names founded on mineral or fossiliferous terms failed to satisfy and that fanciful Greek names were still worse'. So, remembering that the region had been inhabited by a Welsh tribe called the Silures, once led by 'old British Caractacus', he called the rocks that he was mapping and describing in detail the Upper and Lower Silurian systems.

Snowdon, North Wales, 3,560 ft

The most ancient rocks of Britain

On being appointed Professor of Geology at Cambridge, the Reverend Adam Sedgwick declared that though he knew absolutely nothing about the science, his only rival knew a great deal – but it was all wrong. The more he studied the subject, however, the more enthusiastic he was about it, and he worked in several areas with Murchison, the two becoming close friends.

He also investigated the very perplexing structure of the grauwacke in the Lake District. As interspersed among the hardened beds of marine sediment he found strata of volcanic origin, he not only elucidated the geology of the region but made an important advance in the study of volcanicity.

When, like Murchison, he began work in 1831 on the rocks of Wales, Sedgwick deliberately chose those in the north, where they rose highest and were most complicated. Involved though their arrangement was, he succeeded in ascertaining their structure and the order in which they had been formed.

Though he claimed that he had freed himself from the

'Wernerian nonsense' he had learned when he began studying geology, Sedgwick worked both in the Lakes and in North Wales on almost Wernerian lines. Making little use of the fossils that he collected, he based his classification of rocks on their mineral structure. This made it impossible, for the time being, to correlate his strata with similar rock beds in other regions.

He, however, made it quite clear that the rocks of North Wales were far more ancient than the Old Red Sandstone, whose beds ran across their upturned edges. He made it clear too that they were older than the Silurian rocks of South Wales, the uppermost of which were actually in contact with the lowest beds of the Sandstone.

Though Sedgwick and Murchison were agreed on the comparative ages of the two series of rocks, they could not decide upon the exact boundary between them. Having named his own beds, Murchison urged Sedgwick to find a suitable term for the rocks which he had been the first to study. At last the Roman name for Wales, Cambria, was used as a basis, and these rocks, then thought to be the most ancient in Britain, were called the Lower, Middle, and Upper Cambrian system.

Based on an illustration from Murchison's *Siluria* showing a section across the Snowdon Range

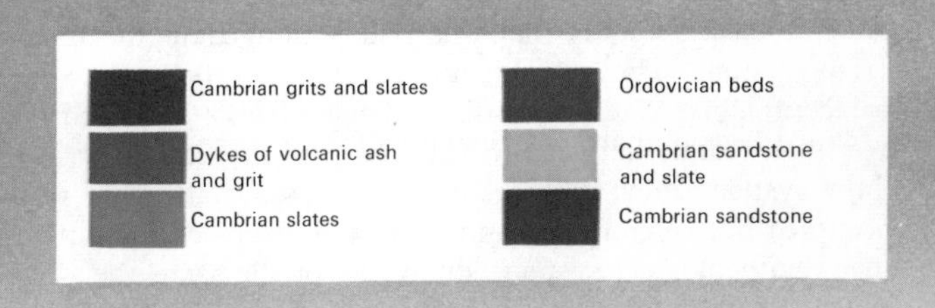

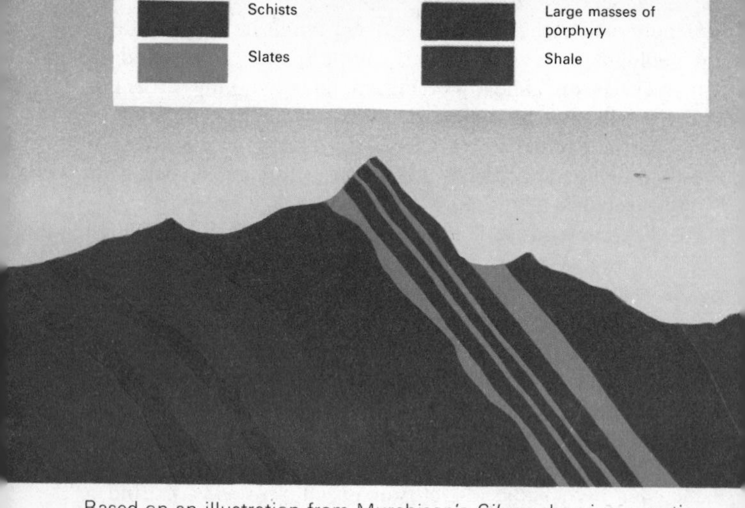

Based on an illustration from Murchison's *Siluria* showing a section across Cader Idris, within the rocks claimed by Sedgwick and Murchison as Silurian, and now classified as Ordovician

The two synchronous systems

The rocks of Devon and Cornwall perplexed even Sedgwick and Murchison. The local grauwacke resembled that of Wales and was even more crushed and contorted yet, unlike the Welsh beds that they had investigated, it contained the fossil remains of plants.

After much thought the two colleagues decided on mineralogical grounds that this rock belonged to the Cambrian system. They could not accept the theory of the palaeontologist William Lonsdale that its fossils indicated an age intermediate between the Silurian and the Carboniferous – the system which includes coal measures. That period was occupied by the Old Red Sandstone, and it seemed incredible that two geological systems should be of the same age.

Two years' further study convinced Sedgwick and Murchison that Lonsdale was right. About a hundred miles apart are two distinct series of rocks, differing completely in mineral character and in the type of fossils that they contain and yet both of the same age!

The two series had in fact been formed under very different conditions, those of Devon and Cornwall beneath the sea and those of southern central Wales in the freshwater inlets or lakes on dry land. For this reason two names were needed to cover one period on the geological time chart. Between the Silurian and the Carboniferous systems comes the Devonian and Old Red Sandstone.

The intercalated system

As Murchison worked backward in time through the Silurian rocks and Sedgwick forward through the older Cambrian, it was inevitable that both should claim some intermediate beds that might reasonably be assigned to either system. When the Geological Survey classed these ambiguous strata as Silurian, Sedgwick, who regarded them as Cambrian, was so deeply offended that his long friendship with Murchison came to an end. This was a sad blow to geology, for their later contributions would have been even more valuable if they had continued to work in partnership. The status of these rocks was not settled until 1879, when Charles Lapworth named them after another Welsh tribe as the Ordovician system.

Cader Idris, Wales, an immense ridge reaching 2,927ft

Research in America

Attracted by the opportunities for research offered by the vast extent of North America, a number of geologists trained in Europe set out across the Atlantic. The United States and Canada at first consisted only of the eastern part of the continent, and it was in those regions that investigation began, soon of course to be continued westwards by geologists born in the New World.

William Maclure, whose map was published in 1817 with a memoir of the region it covered, was hailed as the 'Father of American Geology'. His results were amplified or corrected by other workers over a period of time, so that at last each of the States in the Union had its own Geological Survey. Lardner Vanuxem, whose work on the survey of New York State was especially valuable, correlated some of the American formations with those of Europe by making a comparison of their fossils.

Pioneer studies of eastern Canada were made at this time by officers of the Royal Navy and the Royal Engineers, and here the outstanding achievement was that of William Edmond Logan. About the middle of the nineteenth century, in the course of his studies he discovered an immense geological formation that was far older than the most ancient of the so-called primary rocks. It is known from its shape as the Canadian Shield, and it extends from Hudson's Bay to the line of rivers and lakes that stretches westwards from the St Lawrence River almost to the Rockies.

These investigations were carried out in vast unknown regions and involved much hardship and risk. One of the greatest feats of geological exploration was that accomplished in 1869 by Major John Wesley Powell. Although crippled by the loss during the American Civil War of his right arm, he headed a team of naturalists – three of whom were slain by Red Indians – in a cruise down the Grand Canyon.

In order to co-ordinate the work of such expeditions, the Geological Survey of the United States was established in 1879. Two years later Major Powell was appointed director.

The Grand Canyon, Arizona, is about 200 miles long. Cut by the Colorado River, the canyon shows river erosion on a grand scale.

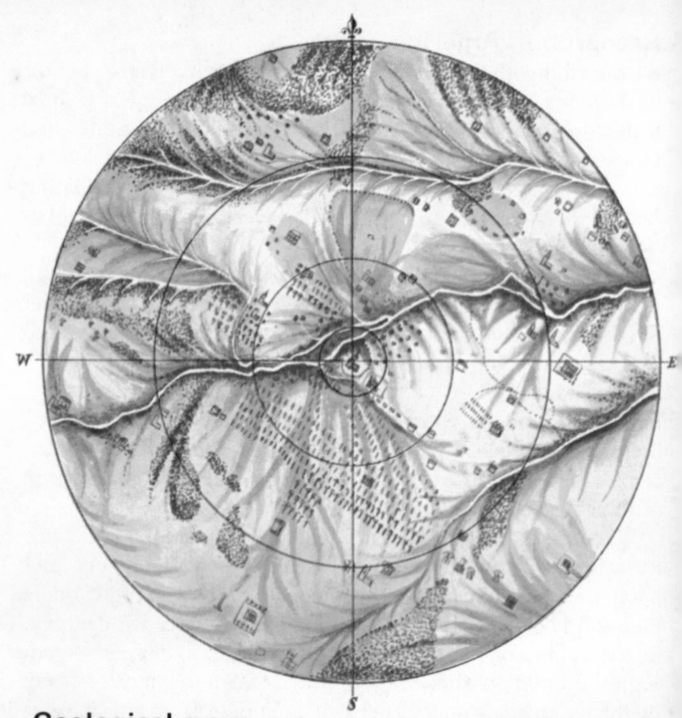

Geological maps

'The industry of future times' amply fulfilled Martin Lister's hopes for 'a new sort of . . . soile or mineral map', for such maps are now being published in greater detail and with greater accuracy than he could have thought possible.

One the earliest was 'A new Philosophical-Chorographical Chart of East Kent, invented and delineated by Christopher Packe, M.D.'. It appeared in 1743 and preceded Guettard's maps by several years. Such pioneer work showed only rock outcrops which in 1775 began to be distinguished by colour. It was William Smith who, in 1815, indicated not merely the outcrops of formations but their structure and age.

Although several Fellows of the Geological Society were interested in Smith's project, the Society itself gave him no help, as it was sponsoring another map upon which one of its founders, G. B. Greenough, was engaged. Published in 1819, this map was on a smaller scale than that of Smith but gave more information about the older systems. About twenty years later, several other geological maps were produced independently – of Scotland by John MacCullough and of Ireland by Richard Griffith. The first map of France was, however, prepared on the same lines as Greenough's.

Far more ambitious was the project of William Maclure, whose map, compiled in 1817, included what was then the whole of the United States. From the eastern seaboard to beyond the Great Lakes and the Mississippi, it indicated on a scale of 120 miles to the inch the outcrops of the larger Wernerian formations. Maclure was not a true Neptunian, but regarded this as the most convenient basis available.

A small-scale map of the world appeared in 1817 under the auspices of the Société Géologique de la France. This too was compiled on Neptunian lines but a larger, more orthodox, world map was produced by the geologist Marcon in 1861.

Packe's Philosophical Chart showing the region around Canterbury (*left*) ; the brown represents arable land, the green, marshes and downland. He meant it to include 'Whatever is Curious, both in Nature and Art that Diversifies and Adorns the Face of the Earth'. (*Below*) modern simplified geological map of Wales

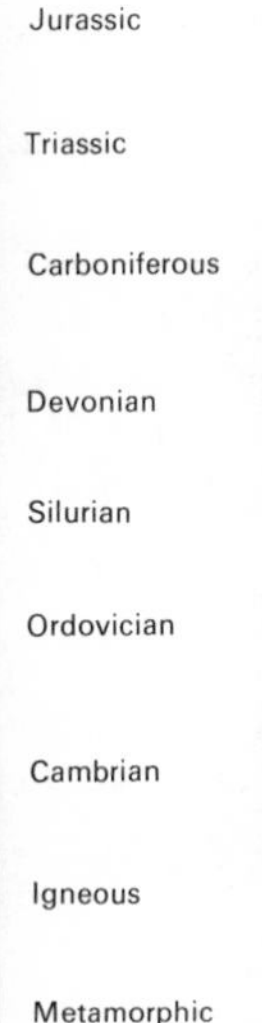

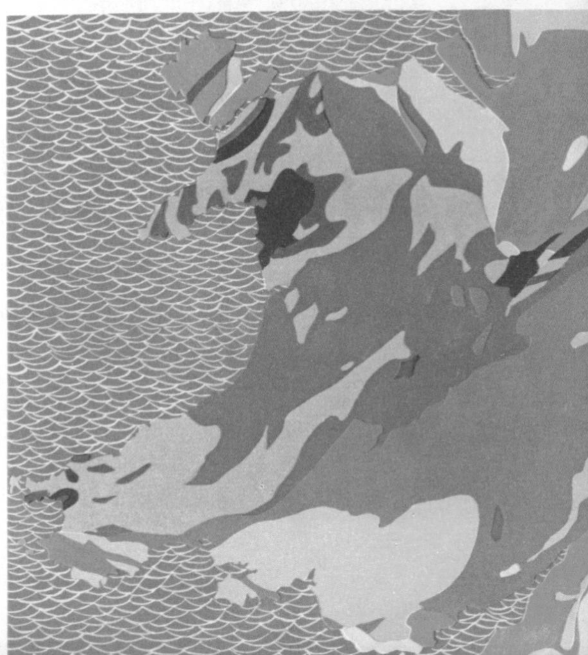

The Geological Survey

William Smith's achievement in mapping the geology of Somerset led to the proposal that he should join the British Ordnance Survey. This suggestion was never acted on, however, and when twenty years later the Geological Survey was formed it was thanks to the efforts of Henry Thomas De la Beche.

The survey was the second institution for scientific research to be established in Britain, the first being the Royal Observatory. Founded in 1836, it is the oldest geological survey in the world, and it formed a model for similar organizations in other lands.

Originally attached to the Ordnance Survey, it soon passed under civil control, so that its officers had no longer to wear a special uniform when in the field! It is now incorporated into the Institute of Geological Sciences, a component body of the Natural Environment Research Council.

Its primary task was to represent in bold outline the geological formations on the one-inch Ordnance Survey maps, colour at first being added by hand. It has now surveyed the greater part of the British Isles on a scale of six inches to the mile, this scale being used on the published maps of such economically-important regions as the coalfields. For the whole of Great Britain, colour maps are also published on a scale ranging from one inch to the mile to twenty-five miles to the inch, the former including vertical and horizontal sections and affording much technical information.

The Survey, which also produces regional memoirs and other more specialized publications, makes a wealth of information available to the enquirer on subjects ranging from Britain's underground water supplies to the minerals used in generating atomic energy.

Almost from the outset it has possessed a Geological Museum, and this, with the Survey headquarters, is now situated in South Kensington, London. It includes an admirable collection of mineral specimens and a number of dioramas and other models illustrating features of special interest. It organizes lectures and demonstrations, which are open to the public.

Typical dress of early nineteenth (*left*) and twentieth-century geologists (*right*)

Glacial action in Britain?

Louis Agassiz, an experienced geologist renowned for his work on fossil fish, was surprised when, about 1836, two of his friends declared that the great boulders on the lower slopes of the Swiss mountains had been transported into their unlikely situations not, as was generally thought, by water but by moving ice. The implication was that glaciers had formerly been far more extensive than they are now, and he thought this improbable.

Hutton and Playfair, among others, had glanced at this theory, but Agassiz, when once he was convinced of its truth, was the first to follow it up in detail. The evidence of former glaciation, he found, is far more widespread than had first seemed possible. Far below the present snow-line, rocks are polished and scored with parallel lines where moving ice has smoothed them and rasped them with sand and grit; and there are masses of loose material, similar to moraines.

Agassiz detected similar evidence elsewhere in northern Europe; and Buckland, though at first incredulous, was convinced when he studied the facts at first hand and realized that he had seen them himself in Scotland.

At his invitation, Agassiz visited Britain in 1840. Almost on his arrival in Glasgow, he detected unmistakable traces of glaciation, and the further he travelled into the Highlands the more obvious these were. Here too the rocks are smoothed and striated; here too are former moraines; here too erratic blocks of stone are perched in places where nothing but moving ice could have taken them. Though for a time they might regard Agassiz' glacial theory as absurd, at last even the most sceptical of British geologists had to admit its truth.

The most striking evidence of glacial action consists of the 'parallel roads of Glenroy', three horizontal terraces running at different levels round a Scottish loch. These former water-lines had formerly been attributed to the results of the Flood or some other inundation. Agassiz explained them convincingly as having been produced when the lake's outlet had been dammed by glaciers that had long since melted away.

Based on a sketch by Agassiz used in connection with his early studies of glaciation, probably about 1841

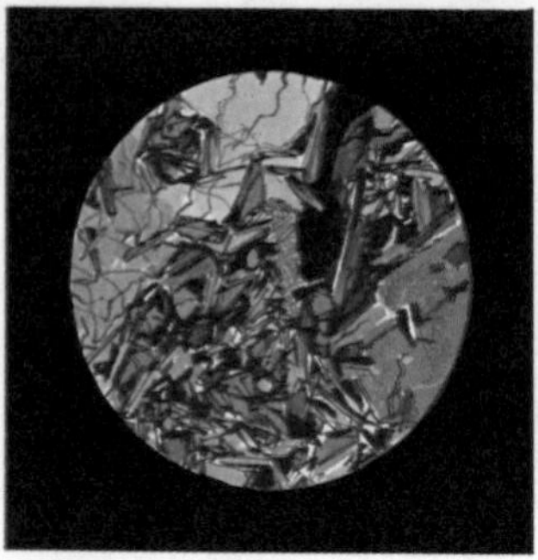

Dolerite

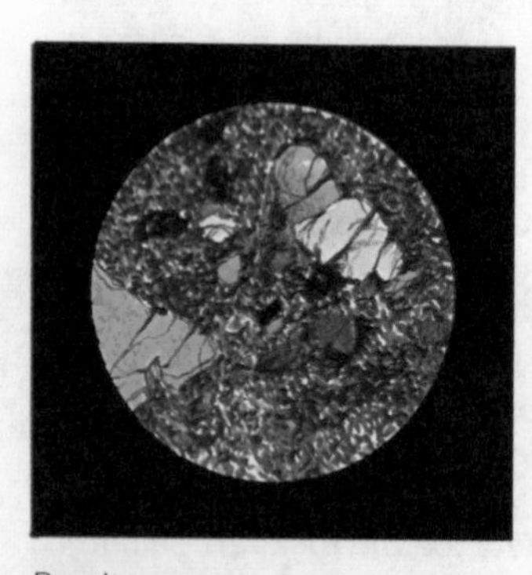

Basalt

Gabbro

The hidden glory of the rocks

Thanks to Werner's brilliance as a mineralogist, Germany was for some time foremost in petrology, the study of the internal structure of the rocks. Nevertheless, progress everywhere was slow. Even if a rock were powdered and examined with a microscope, the various particles could barely be identified.

Advance became possible when, in about 1827, William Nicol, famous for the prism that bears his name, devised a new method of studying fossil wood. By cutting a thin slice of the wood, polishing it, mounting it on a glass slide, and grinding it down into a transparent film, he examined it by transmitted light under the microscope.

Although in 1831 many of his specimens were described in Henry Witham's *Observations on Fossil Vegetables*, little notice was otherwise taken of his work. But his method could also be used on slices of rock and a collection of these slices was studied by H. C. Scorby.

Scorby was especially impressed by the 'fluid cavities' which some of these rock slices contain. In a memoir dated 1858 *On the Micro-*

scopic Structure of Crystals, he explained that this method of investigation throws a new light on the internal structure and composition of the rocks and the conditions in which they were formed.

Lest the objection be raised that it is impossible to look at a mountain through a microscope, he pointed out that 'there is no necessary connection between the size of an object and the value of a fact', and declared that the microscope could render good service in geology.

The Nicol prism, which its inventor described in 1829, consists of two specially-cut pieces of Iceland spar, a form of calcite. Placed between these, a rock section can be examined by polarized light; while yielding further information about the rock's composition and structure, its constituent minerals often appear in beautiful colours. Thinkers of an earlier age might have found a deep religious significance, a new demonstration of the Creator's handiwork, in the revelation of this blaze of glorious colour, hidden deep in the heart of the rocks.

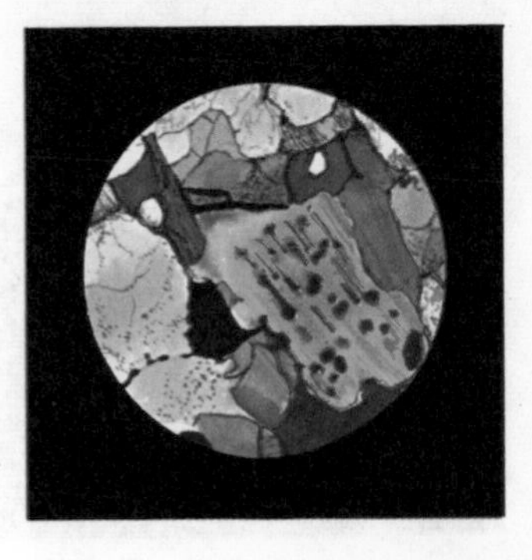

Granite

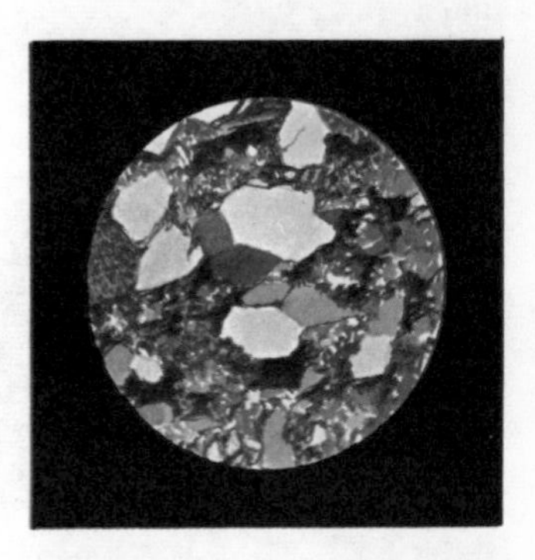

Greywacke

Diorite

Thin sections of rock, as seen by polarized light

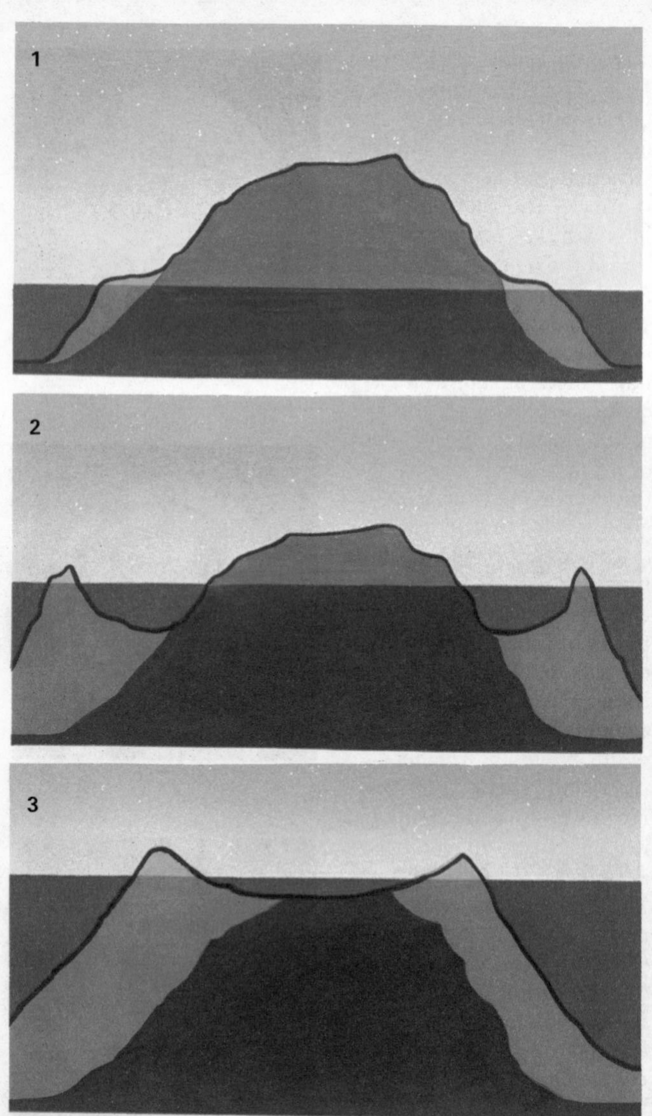

Formation of an atoll: 1. top of submarine mountain forms an island with *fringing reef*; 2. island somewhat submerged is encircled by a *barrier reef*; 3. sunken island is covered by coral which forms an *atoll*, a reef surrounding a central lagoon.

DEVELOPMENTS IN NATURAL HISTORY

Coral reefs and atolls

When, in 1831, the brig *Beagle* was sent by the British Government to make a survey of Southern America, the naturalist attached to the mission was Charles Robert Darwin.

A keen biologist, Darwin had at first found geology intolerably dull, but later he had become enthusiastic about the science, and he accompanied Sedgwick on one of his visits to North Wales. Realizing the great superiority of Lyell's uniformitarianism to the older theories, he took the *Principles of Geology* with him on the *Beagle* and used it as a basis for his own investigations. They included an enquiry into what had been regarded as something of a mystery, the origin of coral reefs. Coral itself was known to consist of the 'skeletons' of tiny marine animals akin to the sea-anemone – but how could these skeletons accumulate to build *fringing* reefs extending outwards from a shore, *barrier* reefs separated from a shore by a channel, and *atolls* in which a ring of reefs surrounds a central lagoon?

The German naturalist Adalbert von Chamisso had surmised that the reefs had been formed on the upper slopes of submarine mountains and had then grown outwards, to form a ring of coral round a lagoon. As, however, coral animals live only in shallow water this hardly seemed probable.

Darwin's study of the reefs suggested a different theory, that the coral had been formed on land that was slowly sinking into the sea. It would at first produce a fringing reef; as the land sank the coral animals would build upwards on the 'dead' coral below to form a barrier reef; when all the land had sunk below sea level, the reefs would constitute an atoll.

Later research has generally confirmed this theory, as modified by Daly's suggestion that the reefs may have been formed, not through actual land subsidence but through a general rise in the sea level caused by melting of the ice sheets at the end of the glacial period, producing the same result. Some of the larger reefs might have been formed by a combination of the two processes.

Evolution by natural selection

Darwin regarded the voyage of the *Beagle* as the most important event of his life. He was already attracted to the idea of evolution – his own grandfather Erasmus Darwin had to some extent anticipated the theories of Lamarck. Now his observations of animal life in the tropics made him feel that evolution had in fact occurred, though as yet he could not imagine anything that could have caused it.

The forebodings of the Reverend Thomas Malthus, that the world is threatened by over-population, made Darwin realize the incessant struggle for existence that prevails among all living creatures. More come into the world than can possibly survive; the great majority are either slain or die prematurely from lack of food or some other natural cause.

Any creature which in some respects is better fitted to survive than its fellows, Darwin realized, is more likely to survive. Then it may hand on to its offspring whatever difference it was that had made its survival possible. So, he inferred, the slow piling-up through the ages of a succession of even small differences might eventually transform it completely into a different type of creature.

During a visit to Malaya in 1858, Wallace first formulated the theory of evolution.

He began work on this theory in 1842 and he was still engaged on it when, in 1858, he was amazed to receive a letter from his friend, the naturalist Alfred Russell Wallace. While collecting zoological specimens in Malaya, Wallace had hit on the same theory and he was curious to know what Darwin thought of it.

Anxious to do justice both to Wallace and to himself, Darwin consulted the geologist Lyell and the botanist Sir Joseph Hooker. On their advice he prepared a summary of his own theory and this was read, together with the communication from Wallace, to the Linnean Society. Wallace agreed that he had acted quite correctly, and there was never any dispute between them regarding priority.

Darwin's statement of his theory, *On the Origin of Species by means of Natural Selection*, appeared in 1859. In 1871 it was followed by his book on human evolution, *The Descent of Man*.

In South America (*right*) Darwin had observed its strange animal life and reached the same conclusions some twenty years earlier.

Man did not, of course, evolve from an ape, but apes and men did diverge from a common ancestral group. Very early forms (*above*) were ape-like in form with a tendency to a bipedal posture.

'There is grandeur in this view of life'

The publication of the *Origin of Species* aroused worldwide controversy. Many biologists doubted whether natural selection could produce such far-reaching results.

Darwin fully realized the difficulties of his theory and discussed them at length. He never claimed that natural selection could be *solely* responsible for evolution, nor did he ignore the possibility that the processes akin to those stressed by Lamarck might have accelerated it. He suspected too, wrongly as more recent research has shown, that if some creature developed a new characteristic this might be 'swamped' by cross-breeding with similar creatures that had not developed it.

In spite of all the arguments it aroused, Darwin's work had transformed evolution from a highly-doubtful hypothesis into an extremely probable theory. Whatever its cause, it is now accepted as a fact by most, if not all, biologists, and it has transformed our whole outlook.

It has especially transformed that of the geologists. It made them realize, as never before, the great imperfection of 'the record of the rocks', the story of life as revealed by the fossils, as well as the unsuspected duration of the whole period of geological time. Above all, it threw a new light upon their work when fossils were regarded as evidence not of separate 'bursts' of creation but of one age-long ever-developing succession of life.

Darwin was hotly attacked not on scientific, but on theological grounds. Unperturbed he carried on with his work, leaving his assailants to be answered by his colleague, Thomas Huxley.

To some thinkers this theory seemed more irreligious than uniformitarianism itself. It seemed to deny the belief that the Earth and its inhabitants had been created through Divine action.

But to Darwin himself it afforded evidence of Divine action. As he put it at the conclusion of *The Origin of Species*: 'There is grandeur in this view of life, with its several powers, having been originally breathed by the Creator into a few forms or one; and that . . . from so simple a beginning, endless forms most beautiful and wonderful have been, and are being, evolved.'

The first recognizable form is *Australopithecus* (*bottom left*) who lived in caves and had an upright stance. Early races of modern man (*below*) are called Cro-Magnon man (*above*) and evolved about 25,000 years ago

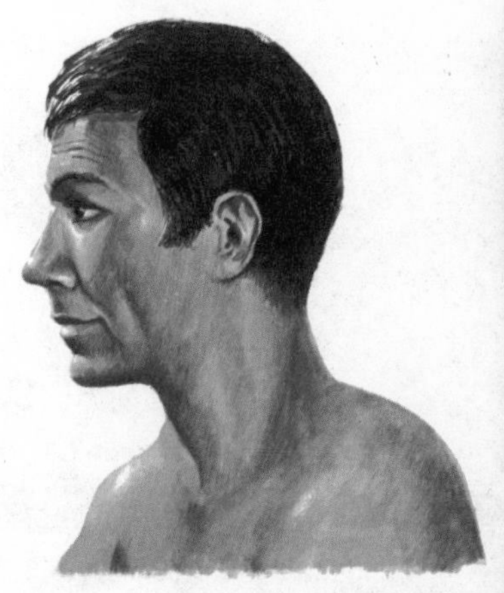

THE EARTH TODAY

The weather and the rocks

Although great progress in geology was made during the early nineteenth century, one branch of the science was comparatively neglected: geomorphology, the study of the forces which mould the Earth's surface.

The weather has always forced itself upon human attention but only in modern times has it been studied systematically. The first meteorological instrument may have been Galileo's device for measuring the air temperature, the forerunner not only of the thermometer but of the barometer. Modern methods of studying weather include the launching into the upper air of meteorological instruments that are carried by radio sonde balloons, high-altitude rockets, and artificial satellites.

These show that the atmosphere extends thousands of miles above the Earth's surface, decreasing in density with height until it 'peters out' into the comparative emptiness of space, and comprising several 'layers' in which conditions differ greatly. It shields the Earth by burning up almost all of the meteors which bombard it from space and it tempers the intensity of the sunshine and the cosmic rays.

A network of weather observing stations far out to sea is provided by specially-equipped weather ships. They report four to eight times daily like ordinary land stations.

The air consists of a complex mixture of gases, about one-fifth oxygen and four-fifths nitrogen, with smaller quantities of such inert gases as argon, and of carbon dioxide and water vapour. It also contains varying amounts of material derived from the earth and sea and their inhabitants: salt, dust particles, decaying matter, seeds, pollen and bacteria, and such by-products of human activity as smoke, industrial gases and atomic waste. It interpenetrates the sea and other stretches of water as bubbles and in solution; the earth, in caves and other crevices; and all living creatures as their breath.

The atmosphere forms an important agent of geological erosion. Its changes of temperature wear the rocks away and its dust-laden wind blows away their fragments. The rain not only washes those fragments of rock away, but actually dissolves the rocks' surface, for it consists not of pure water but of a weak but nevertheless effective solution of carbonic acid.

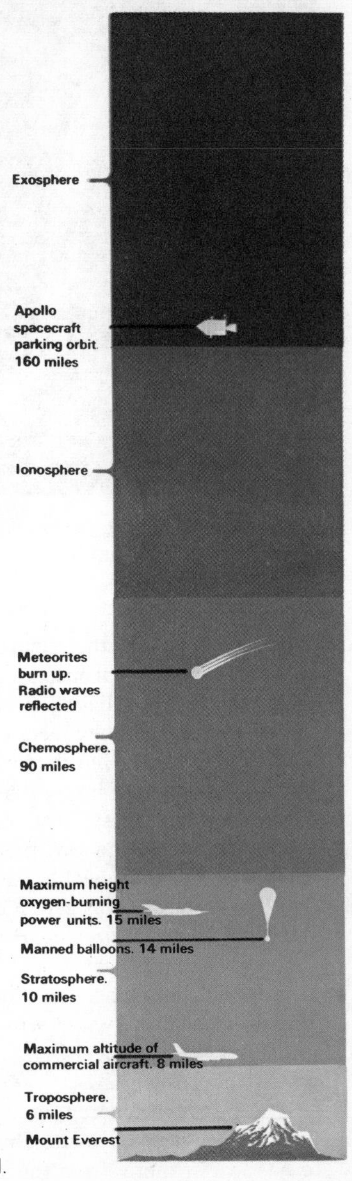

The structure of the Earth's atmosphere showing the different layers and heights above sea level.

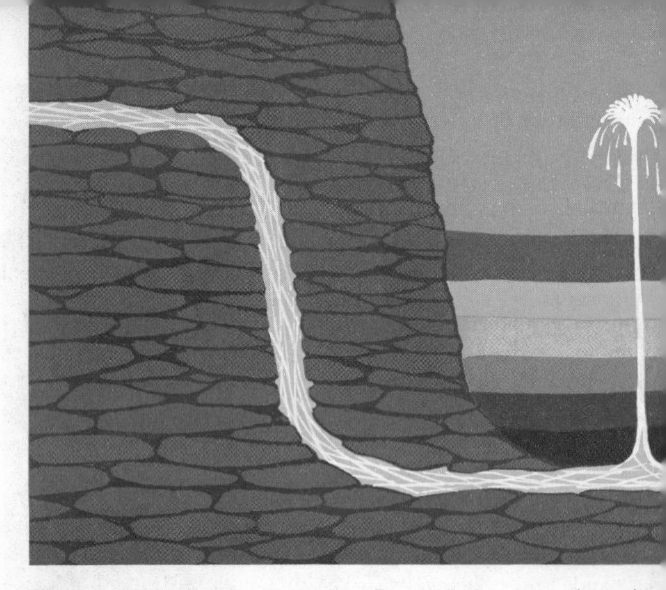

Based on an illustration designed by Ramazzini to explain the action of the Artesian Wells at Modena

Flowing water

When interest in the structure of scenery revived, on subject especially aroused controversy: the origin of th river valleys. Had the valleys decided the direction taken b the rivers, or had the rivers excavated the valleys?

For a long time, even the idea that rivers could be produce by the rain seemed incredible. Only in 1580 did the Frenc master-potter Palissy declare that rain is generated b evaporation from the sea; that seeping into the ground unti it reaches an impermeable surface of rock and oozing dow over the surface of this bed, it emerges as springs, the essentia source of even the greatest rivers.

About a century later, in 1691, the Italian Ramazzini gav a graphic description of the artesian wells at Modena explaining that the water which feeds them had accumulate underground at a level higher than that of the sources fror which they flow.

It seemed even more incredible that the great river valley had literally been excavated by the rivers. They were though to have been there 'from the beginning', or attributed to th

forces which produced 'Noah's Flood', or to catastrophic earth movements, or to 'tidal waves' sweeping in from the sea, or to the continued action of more ordinary waves and currents, or to sea currents operating when the region was submerged.

At last, however, the destructive effect was realized, not so much of flowing water itself as of the solid material which it rasps against the rocks over which it flows. In hard rocks this material scrapes downward, cutting the river floor ever deeper until it may trench the rocks with a narrow canyon. In softer beds it works not so much downwards as sideways, changing its direction repeatedly and producing a broad, shallow valley far wider than the stream itself.

Meanwhile the material swept along by the rivers has been worn down into silt and, when the force of the current slackens, this silt is deposited along its banks to form the wide alluvial plains which border river mouths, or is swept out to sea by the ebb of the tides.

Flowing water thus acts partly as a chisel to groove the land with valleys and partly as a plane to smooth it. If nothing interfered with this process, it might in time reduce a mountain to a featureless mass of silt just above sea level.

Underground water

Caverns have always evoked awe and aroused curiosity, and the Greek thinkers, impressed at seeing streams vanishing into some caves and emerging from others, naturally inferred the existence of unseen rivers flowing underground.

Caves have served as homes and refuges throughout history, but no report of their investigation was published until 1535; the earliest comprehensive account of the caves then accessible is *The Underground World*, compiled during the seventeenth century by the French scholar Jacques Gaffarel. Only in recent times has the systematic study of caves become a science, called speleology, and their exploration a sport, 'mountaineering in reverse'.

The more important caves were excavated by the carbonic acid contained in even the purest water; this dissolves the calcite of which chalk and limestone are formed. The underground watercourses thus produced mostly follow the dip of the rock beds, though they may also cut swallow-holes downwards through weak places in the rock. If the flow of water slackens, its channel may dry up to form a cave.

Few caves are completely dry, however, and the water flowing or seeping through them evaporates and deposits its minerals as a stony crust. Hence the striking features of many caverns, the gleaming dripstone lining the walls, the stalactites and stalagmites growing downwards and rising upwards from the roof and floor and building impressive columns.

Bones of hyaenas and other animals found on the cave floors were regarded as evidence of Noah's Flood by Dr Buckland – described by Dr Gordon L. Davies, in his book *The Earth in Decay*, as being entitled to 'the doubtful honour of being the last British geologist of note to relate the discoveries of modern geology to the Mosaic writings'.

Sub-human and human remains have also been unearthed in rock shelters and the walls and roofs of some large caverns have been decorated, presumably for magical reasons, with magnificent drawings and paintings of prehistoric animals made by contemporary artists.

The striking features of a cave in a limestone area. Stalactites grow towards the floor and stalagmites rise to meet them.

Glaciers

No sooner was Louis Agassiz' theory of glacial action accepted than evidence in its favour was found in many parts of the world and in several distinct geological formations; they even occurred in the primeval rocks of the Canadian Shield.

There have, in fact, been at least four periods of glaciation. The most recent of these was the Great Ice Age which lasted for about a million years and ended over 20,000 years ago. During this time, the polar ice cap extended across Britain down to the Thames, across Europe into central France and the Alps, and across America as far as the Great Lakes. Even further to the south mountain heights were snow-clad, and there was also much glaciation in parts of the southern hemisphere.

The cause of the glacial periods is uncertain. Among the theories suggested are fluctuations in the heat of the Sun, variations in the Earth's orbit, and changes in the outlines or levels of sea and land – a gap between the two Americas, for example, would divert the warm waters of the Gulf Stream into the Pacific.

Whatever its cause, the Great Ice Age had far-reaching effects upon the earth and its plant and animal life. The glaciers scoured valleys and excavated lakes, dammed or diverted rivers, and transported great boulders and masses

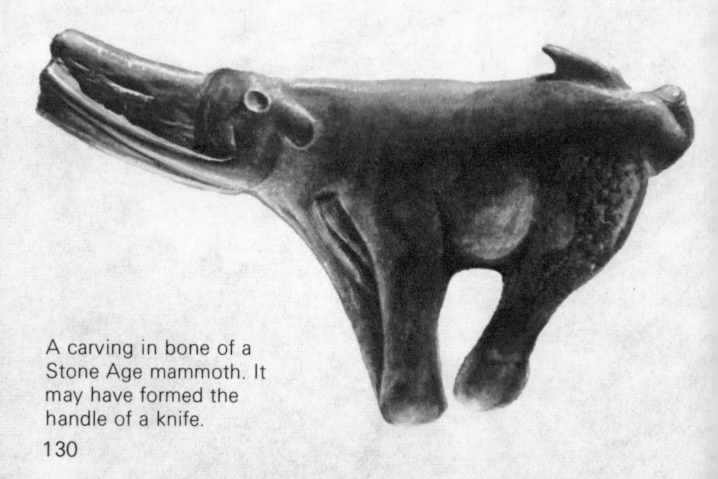

A carving in bone of a Stone Age mammoth. It may have formed the handle of a knife.

Cave drawings, also Stone Age, from the cavern of Niaux in the Pyrenees

of loose material far across the land. Living creatures unable to endure or elude the cold perished; the only survivors were those animals that were able to withstand the rigours of the climate.

However, these rigours were not continuous during the Great Ice Age, as there were Glacial Periods of intense cold separated by Interglacial Periods of comparative warmth. It is uncertain whether the Great Ice Age is now passing away, so that we may hope for milder conditions, or whether a Fourth Interglacial Period is ending, confronting us with the prospect of a return of the ice.

It was towards the end of the Third Interglacial Period that human life appeared. The first inhabitants of western Europe lived during the early Stone Age; the animals depicted on cave walls, which include the woolly mammoth and the bison and reindeer, testify to the cold conditions of the last Glacial Period in which they lived.

The sea

Not until the third day of Creation, the Bible asserts, did the dry land appear; and the belief that the Earth was completely covered by water long swayed geological speculation and may possibly have influenced Werner's Neptunian theories.

Now covering three-quarters of the Earth's surface, the sea consists of brine, fed by the rivers, which in turn are fed by the rain derived from the sea's evaporation. It is rendered increasingly salt by the material that the rivers dissolve from the rocks. The sea is always in motion. Its convection currents mingle water from different levels; its waves are produced by the thrust of the wind; its tides are produced by the action of the Moon and the Sun; and its currents are produced by the Earth's rotation.

The Ancient Greeks knew of the sea as the 'Earth Shaker'; it is now known to be literally the Earth's destroyer. Its waves pound the shore with masses not only of water but of pebbles and grit. They compress into crannies in the rock volumes of air which expand with tremendous force as the

Coastal erosion will soon destroy not only the cliffs, but the houses upon them.

waves recoil. They swirl loose rock about and grind it into pebbles and sand, which are swept along the shore by currents and tides. In this way the coast is eroded by the sea, and though some of its fragments lodge against the shore and extend it seawards, the small tracts of new land thus formed do not compensate for the vaster masses worn away.

The bulk of the material ripped from the land seeps down to the sea floor. On the shallow continental shelves that surround the land masses, it produces quicksands and sand banks. In the depths further out it accumulates to form an ooze, filled with the skeletons of microscopic animals and plants. In the ocean depths these are destroyed by the brine, and here the sea floor is covered with a red clay.

Thus the sea complements the work of the rivers in destroying the land. Should nothing check or counteract this work, their combined action would complete the process. The Earth would then become what the Bible declares that it originally was, a land mass everywhere covered by the sea.

Based on a model in the London Geological Museum of the Haig Pit in the collieries of Whitehaven, Cumberland

Rocks and rock structures

In geological usage the term *rock* differs from its ordinary meaning. It implies any substance, irrespective of hardness, that forms part of the Earth. All rocks consist of *minerals*, each of which has its own chemical composition and physical characteristics: the word *mineral* means 'things mined' and many minerals are in fact mined because of their economic importance.

Rocks are classified by their origin. The *igneous* (fire-formed) rocks were produced by the cooling down of molten material from within the Earth, and in these rocks minerals occur in the form of crystals. When the cooling took place deep underground it proceeded very gradually and the crystals are large enough to be easily distinguishable; an example is granite, which appears in great masses where the rocks that once covered it have been eroded away. Where the molten material welled up from below through volcanic vents or forced its way up in thin sheets through the other

rocks it cooled more quickly and its crystals, as in basalt, are microscopically small.

The *sedimentary* rocks, as their name implies, were formed under water as sediments derived from the remains of other rocks. Almost all of them are arranged in *strata* (layers). Although they were originally horizontal, or nearly so, these layers have in many places been tilted by earth movements to slope steeply or stand upright, or been bent into *anticlines* (arches) or *synclines* (troughs), and even folded into contortions. Knowledge of these formations is essential to the mining engineer, for coal occurs in such seams, and the oil may saturate a layer of permeable rocks which lie between two impermeable rock beds, and it then finds its way to the top of the anticlines.

Certain rocks, originally igneous or sedimentary, have been so transformed by intense heat or great pressure as to be completely unrecognizable; marble, for example, was formerly a limestone. Such rocks are known as *metamorphic* from Greek words meaning 'changed in form'.

The geological eras and their chief subdivisions with the pioneer geologists associated with them				
Eras	**Periods**	**Age of base**	**Dominant life form**	**Pioneer geologist**
Cenozoic (Quaternary)	Recent (Great Ice Age) Pleistocene	Million years 1	Man	Agassiz
Cenozoic (Tertiary)	Pliocene Miocene Oligocene Eocene	60	Mammals Modern vegetation	Lyell
Mesozoic (Secondary) *Age of reptiles*	Cretaceous	130	Reptiles Conifers Ferns	W. Smith
	Jurassic: Oolite Lias	170	"	W. Smith Mary Anning
	Triassic (New Red Sandstone)	200	"	W. Smith
Upper Palaeozoic (Primary) *Age of amphibians*	Permian (New Red Sandstone)	220	"	Pallas
	Upper Carboniferous (Pennsylvanian coal measures)	260	Swamp Forests	W. Smith
Age of fish	Lower Carboniferous (Mississippian)	280	Amphibians	W. Smith
	Devonian Old Red Sandstone	320	Fish Land Plants	Lonsdale Hugh Miller
Lower Palaeozoic (Primary) *Age of invertebrates*	Silurian	360	Invertebrates Seaweeds	Murchison
	Ordovician	430	"	Lapworth
	Cambrian	520	"	Sedgwick
Pre-Cambrian		3000	Low forms of life	Logan

The record of the rocks

Most sedimentary rocks contain fossils; some limestones, indeed, almost consist of them. As the succession of these rocks – the order in which they were formed – can be ascertained, their fossils give a clue to the development of life on earth.

This development comprises five great Eras. In the very oldest rocks the paucity of fossils suggests that the earliest living creatures, those of the Pre-Cambrian Era, were of very primitive type and almost destitute of any hard parts which could become fossilized.

In what were formerly called the primary rocks, abundant fossils show that during the Primary or Palaeozoic Era (from the Greek for *ancient life*) the sea swarmed at first with such invertebrates as shellfish, starfish and corals and later also with the earliest fish. The period represented by the Upper Palaeozoic rocks could indeed be called the Age of Fish, so numerous are their fossils. During this Period, too, life spread on to the land; it included the first reptiles, as well as the swamp forests whose fossilized remains form coal.

Yet it was the Secondary, or Mesozoic (*middle life*) Era that was the Age of Reptiles, some of which were monstrous in form and size. The huge monsters died out towards the end of the Period, but some smaller forms show indications that they were developing into birds and others into mammals.

The Cenozoic (*recent life*) Era, the greater part of which is also called the Tertiary, was the Age of Mammals. At first large and ungainly, these animals came increasingly to resemble those of the present day. The plants, too, were largely of modern type. Brief though it is, the later part of the Cenozoic Era is classed as a distinct period, for it was during this time that human life developed. The Quaternary Period is, in short, the Age of Man.

The work of William Smith, the first geologist to recognize rocks by their fossils, has now been made much more precise. Many of the sedimentary rocks consist of thin zones, each identifiable by its characteristic fossil. Apart from its practical value in enabling the prospector to realize exactly what rock he is dealing with, this zonation enables the evolution of many living creatures to be worked out in great detail.

Terrestrial magnetism

The strange properties of magnetic iron ore have long been known. In classical Greece the miners, who used this ore, lodestone, to find their way about the workings, thought it magical; and though the thinkers studied it more objectively they could make little of it.

The Chinese, who used lodestone much earlier, are doubtfully credited with the invention of the mariner's compass. This reached Europe in the thirteenth century; the first treatise on its use appeared in 1269. Its variation from true north may have been discovered by Columbus when he crossed the Atlantic in 1492. This discovery seriously alarmed his crew and he had to make several ingenious attempts to bluff them. Salvador de Madariaga, in his biography, refers to the relevant pages in Columbus' 'log'.

The compass was believed to indicate some point within

The solar wind emanating from the sun compresses the Earth's magnetic field on its sunward side, forming the Van Allen belts and producing the aurorae; it also sends a 'tail', 100,000 miles long, streaming from the Earth's farther side.

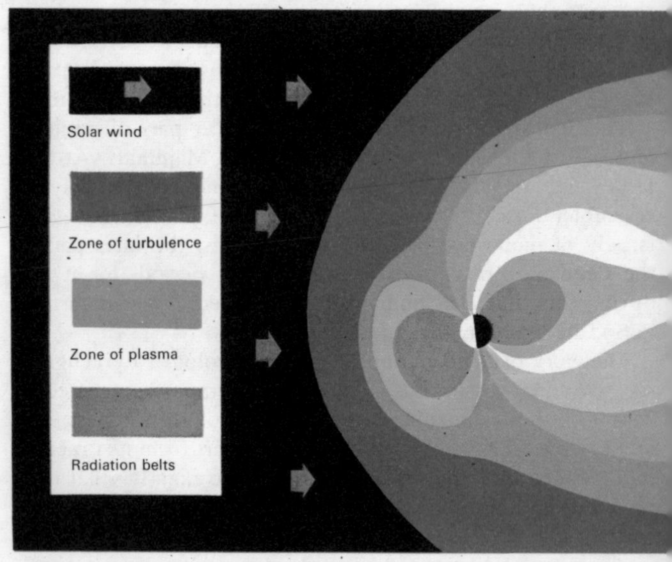

the sky until. in 1576, Robert Norman found that it indicates some point within the earth. By a series of ingenious experiments William Gilbert showed, in about 1600, that the earth itself is an immense magnet. In the nineteenth century the German mathematician Gauss organized the study of geomagnetism at the observatories, and it was realized that the Earth is surrounded by a magnetic field.

While investigating the theory that this magnetic field is produced, dynamo fashion, by the Earth's rotation, the British physicist Runcorn ascertained that certain rocks contain 'fossil magnets'. Specks of iron in flowing lava or in the sediments on the sea floor had been free to move, and they had pointed like tiny compasses towards the magnetic poles at that time. After the lava flow had solidified or the sediment had hardened, they continued to point in the same direction.

These fossils, however, do not indicate the present magnetic north and south. Their directions show that the Earth's magnetic poles have, so to speak, 'wandered' about the polar regions and that the Earth's magnetism has actually been reversed more than once. Such changes may be due to variations in the electrical charges at the Earth's core.

Radioactivity

While investigating fluorescence in 1896, the French physicist Becquerel was amazed to find that some photographic plates, though tightly wrapped up, had become inexplicably 'fogged' in the presence of small quantities of uranium. This element, he surmised, must emit radiations akin to the X-rays recently discovered by Röntgen.

While following up this action the Curies ascertained that much more powerful than the uranium itself were the traces it contained of an element hitherto undiscovered: they called this element radium.

An inquiry into radioactivity led Rutherford to investigate atomic structure. He found that the rays were produced by the disintegration of such elements as uranium, which gradually 'decays' into lead, the process involving the steady generation of heat.

His discoveries threw light on a number of geological problems. Since Buffon it had been assumed that the Earth had long ago been thrown off from the Sun, that it had then

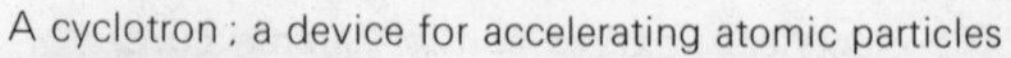
A cyclotron; a device for accelerating atomic particles

been intensely hot, and that, in spite of the heat that still prevailed at its centre, it had since been cooling down from the surface inwards. Lord Kelvin had estimated that the Earth was formed about twenty million years ago – a period which the geologists regarded as being far too short to allow for the evolution of living creatures.

Kelvin had however conceded that the discovery of a new source of heat might modify his figures. Now this new source had been discovered – the heat produced by the disintegration of uranium. While this also accounted for the high temperatures at the Earth's centre, it implied that the Earth is far older than had ever been supposed.

It indeed enabled the age of the various geological formations to be calculated. As the rate at which uranium is transformed into lead is known, the age of any rock bed could be estimated from the proportion within it of these two elements. The probable ages of the basal beds of the geological eras are indicated in the table on page 136; that of the Earth itself is estimated at approximately 4500 million years.

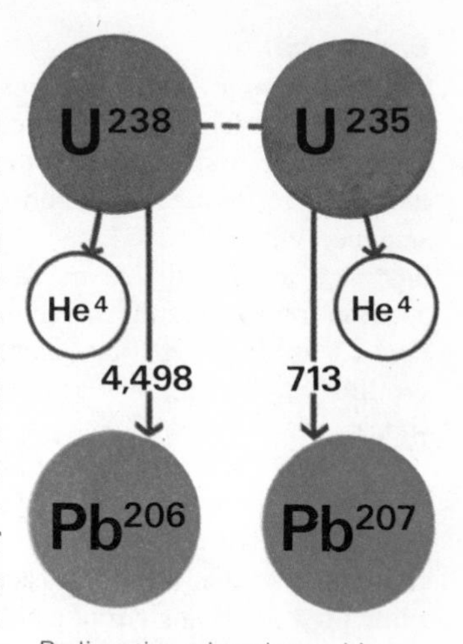

Radioactive minerals used in dating rocks; parent isotopes and half-lives in millions of years with the resulting end products. (*Above*) uranium decays to lead (*below left*) thorium to lead (*right*) rubidium to strontium.

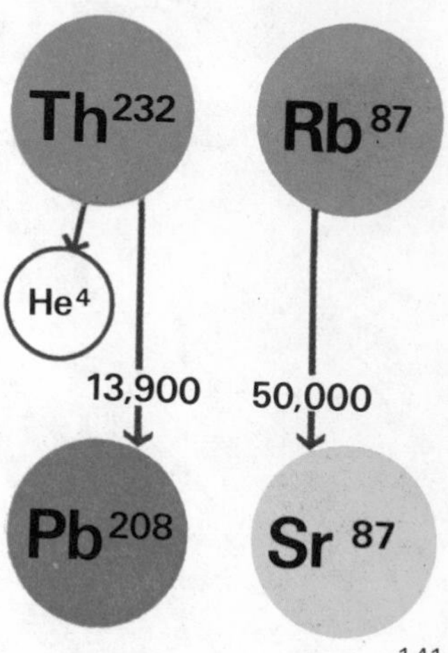

Earthquakes

Lyell's *Principles of Geology* describes the far-reaching effects that earthquakes have produced in the earth's crust. It was however the Irish engineer Robert Mallet who first attempted in 1846, to reduce the study of earthquakes to an exact science; when in 1857 the Naples area was devastated he hastened to visit the scene, afterwards publishing a graphic account of the results of the disaster. Mallet was also the first to produce 'artificial earthquakes' by means of underground explosions in order to study the spread of the shock-waves.

The first instrument for accurately recording natural shock-waves was invented in 1897 by the English seismologist John Milne. His pioneer seismograph consisted of a pendulum supported so that any local earth tremors made a stylus trace a line on a moving strip of smoked paper. Such trails are now recorded photographically by narrow beams of light actuated simultaneously by an 'array' of seismometers, and they are compared on an international basis with those produced elsewhere by the same earthquake.

The records enable the violence and the exact centre of an

earthquake to be ascertained, and they show too that the earth is continually agitated by local tremors so small that they would otherwise go unnoticed. These *microseisms* are produced by traffic, by factory machinery, by rain or frost, by waves breaking on the seashore, and even by cyclones powerful enough to send shocks down through the water to the ocean bed far out at sea.

Artificial seismic shocks generated by explosions are used in geophysical prospecting; by revealing the lie of the rock beds deep underground they obviate the expense of drilling. Thus they may disclose the presence of oil or other minerals or show whether a site is suitable for the construction of a dam.

Seismograph records can also be used for detecting underground and nuclear explosions. To facilitate this, special arrays of seismometers have been set up at Eskdalemuir, Scotland (under the United Kingdom Atomic Energy Authority) and in the United States.

In the San Francisco earthquake (1906) most of the damage was due to fire.

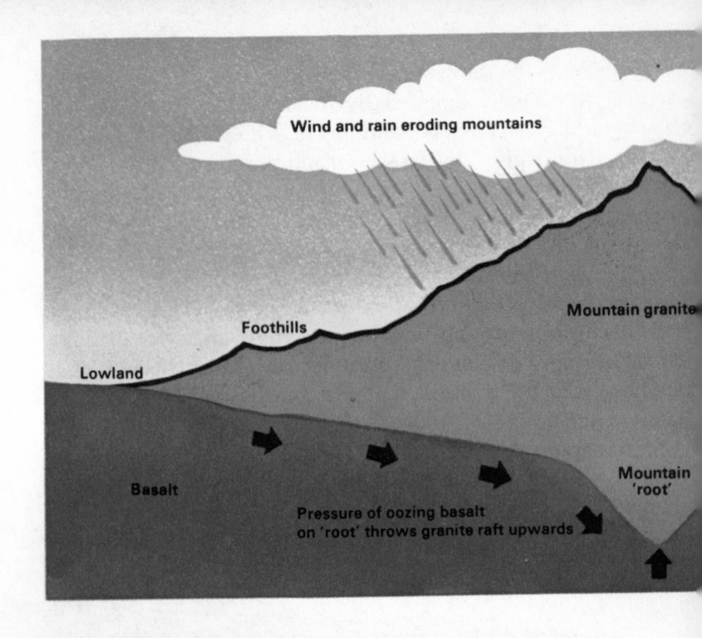

Mountain building

On the theory that the Earth has long been cooling down, the origin of the mountains seemed obvious; they simply resembled 'puckers' formed by the contracting surface of the rocks.

The Earth has not, however, been slowly cooling, nor does the run of the mountain ranges suggest puckering. The mountains are, moreover, more than great rock masses towering above the ground. Measurement of the gravitational forces in their vicinity shows that they have 'roots', that the masses of rock also extend downwards below the ground.

There is evidence, indeed, that the Earth's superficial rocks rest upon great sheets of granite which themselves rest upon an underlying sheet of basalt. The basalt, especially when heated, is slightly plastic and yields sluggishly to great and long-continued pressure, and as the granite is lighter than the basalt it might be compared to a giant raft floating on a plastic sea. The roots of the mountains project downwards from the base of the granite into the basalt. In 1857 the American geologist James Hall made the novel suggestion

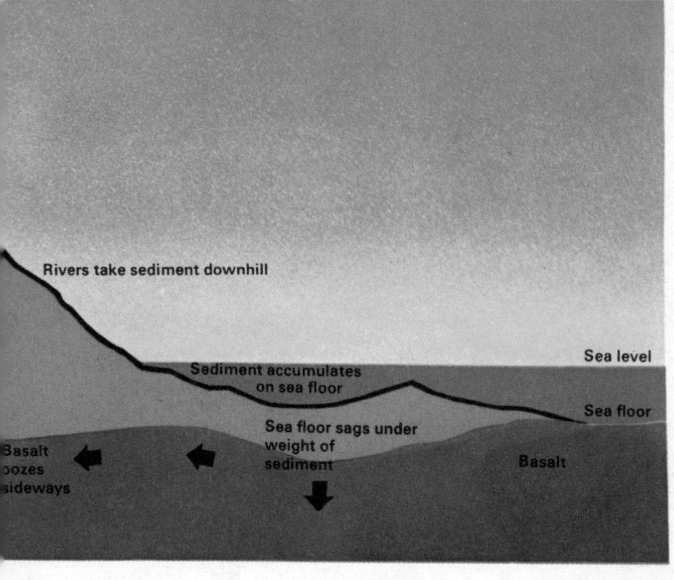

Diagrammatic example of the theory of isostacy

that the material weathered away from the land accumulates as a sediment in the off-shore shallows, where its growing weight forces the sea floor to sag downwards into the basalt.

Then in 1889 Hall's compatriot C. E. Dutton put forward his theory of *isostasy*, that the basalt yields in such a manner as to equalize the pressures upon it. As the sediment accumulates its pressure increases, while the mountains are being slowly eroded away, so that their pressure is diminishing. To compensate for the changing stresses the basalt oozes sideways and presses against the roots of the mountains, forcing them upwards. Thus for some time a mountain retains its original height, its base rising while its crest is destroyed.

The cause of the earth movements that raise the hardened layers of sediment to form new mountain ranges is not yet clear. They might be due to bodily expansion of the basalt as it is slowly heated by the disintegration of the radioactive minerals that it contains. Whatever their cause, there seem to have been half-a-dozen great periods of mountain building, separated by long ages of comparative quiescence.

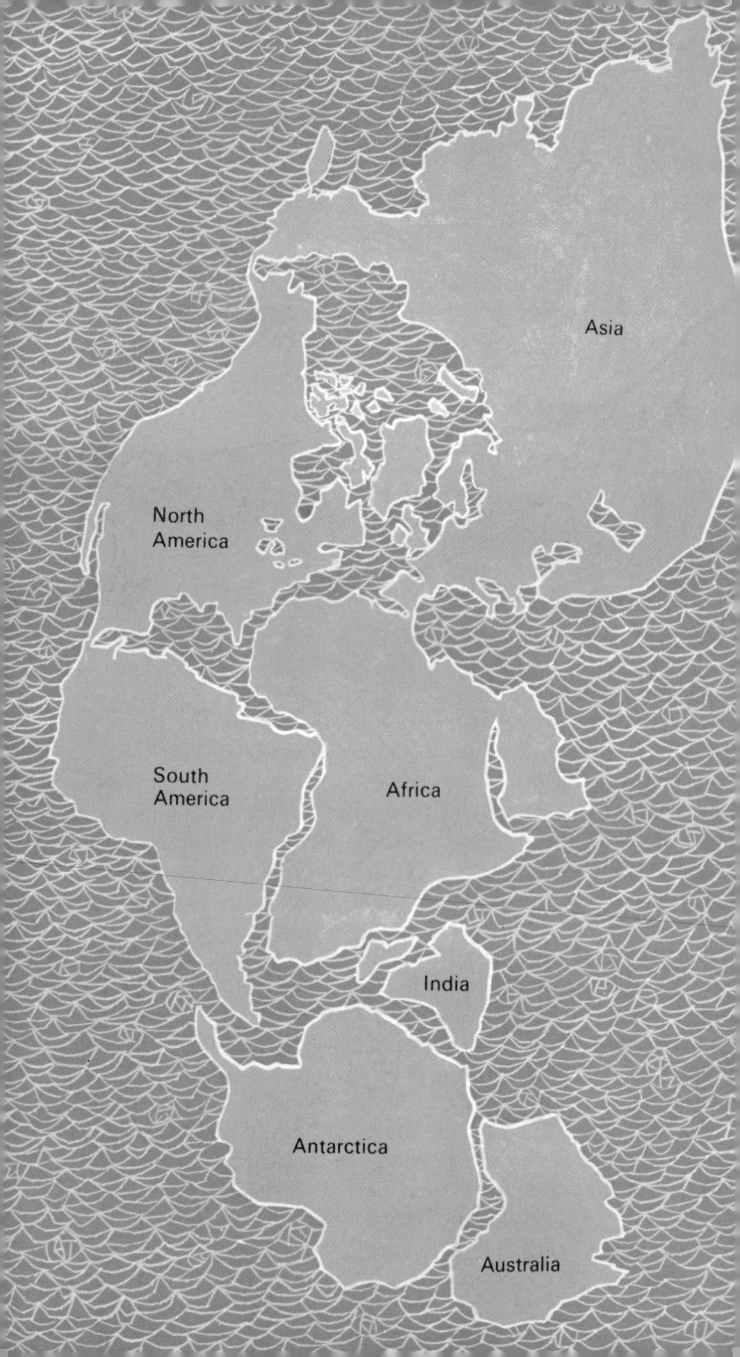
Asia
North
America
South
America
Africa
India
Antarctica
Australia

Continental drift

The strange similarity between the opposite shores of the Atlantic, which look as if they could be fitted together, led the geologists to examine the obvious possibility that they might at one time have been united. The researches of F. B. Taylor enabled him, in 1910, to put forward the theory of world-wide continental drift.

This theory was elaborated by the German scientist Alfred Wegener. Regarding the land masses as resting upon granite rafts floating on a sea of plastic basalt, he pointed out that the Earth's rotation would tend to drive them towards the Equator and that this movement would tend to break them up along lines of weakness. A super-continent near the North Pole, Wegener declared, had drifted southwestwards, fragments breaking off from its eastern coast to form the islands of the Pacific and off Asia. A great mass later drifted further westwards, becoming North America and Greenland.

Another continent at the South Pole split radially into four triangular masses separating from Antarctica. One drifted northwest to become South America and unite with North America; as these moved westwards, the pressure of the basalt against the advancing edges crumpled them to form the Rocky Mountains and the Andes.

Even greater were the mountain ranges produced when what is now the Eurasian continent collided, slowly but with inconceivable force, against two of the triangular land masses advancing from the south. They form the line of mountains extending from Malaysia through the Himalayas and the Caucasus into the Alps. As a result of the collision India became part of the continent; so did Africa, but later this split away along the Red Sea. The fourth southern wedge is now Australia, its detached tip becoming Tasmania.

These mighty earth movements may have been caused by radioactivity. Beneath the land masses, the basalt warmed up and expanded, while between them it was kept cool by the sea. Thus a very gentle slope was formed, and down this the continents slid, the change of temperature producing lines of weakness along which the granite rafts split.

The continents may originally have been joined much as shown.

The interior of the Earth

The deepest mines and boreholes scratch only the surface of the Earth, and the depths have to be investigated by indirect methods. These show that heat and pressure increase with depth, and that the Earth has a central core, probably of nickel-iron surrounded by a 'mantle' of a rock resembling olivine. This result has now been confirmed and amplified by the study of earthquake waves.

For any earthquake, there is a region in which its waves can be recorded. It extends about 105° from the focus over about a quarter of the Earth's circumference. Beyond that limit there is a 'shadow zone' in which the waves are faint and blurred; this extends only to about 140° from the focus, and beyond the zone they can again be recorded clearly.

As R. D. Oldham explained in 1906, the reason that the waves fail to reach the shadow zone is that they are deflected by a core of heavy material at the Earth's centre. The American seismologist Beno Gutenberg was able to measure this core, which he regarded as consisting entirely of molten metal and as being about 4320 miles in diameter.

By the study of the waves that do reach the shadow zone, the Danish seismologist Miss I. Lehmann showed in 1936 that within this core there is an inner core, about 1600 miles across, in which the metal is solid.

An earthquake which occurred in 1910 indicated the existence of what was called, after its Yugoslav discoverer, the Mohorovičić discontinuity (Moho) between the basalt underlying the crust of the Earth and the mantle below. It lies at about five miles below the sea floor and at an average of about twenty miles below the surface of the land. The American Mohole Project, now discontinued, was an attempt to drill a bore through the bed of the Pacific in order to obtain specimens of the mantle itself.

Other researches have disclosed that the ocean bed is literally strewn with countless millions of small manganese nodules; they also contain iron and smaller quantities of nickel, cobalt and other metals. Produced by deposition of the minerals in the sea water, they mostly form in concentric layers round nuclei consisting of such materials as fragments of pumice. They are estimated to be accumulating at the rate

Simplified illustration of a section through the Earth showing its olivine 'mantle' surrounding its central core of a substance resembling nickel-iron. Pressure waves produced by earthquakes are deflected by the difference in density between mantle and core, so that on reaching the latters' surface, they do not traverse the core but are reflected back into the mantle. The result of this deflection is to produce a 'shadow zone' in which the waves of the earthquakes are only recorded very faintly.

of several million tons a year and they, and the sediment on the sea floor, will eventually harden to form new rock beds within the crust of the Earth.

International geophysics and space travel

During the International Geophysical Year, which extended from July 1957 to December 1958, the world's scientists co-operated in systematic research on the physical aspects of the Earth. Among the many achievements during this period, two were outstanding.

The 'Unknown Continent' for which Cook had sought in vain lay, as he surmised, around the South Pole. This is, of course, now called Antarctica and was first reached in 1820. Its coastal regions had already been explored when, in 1911 and 1912, the Pole itself was reached by the expeditions that were led by Amundsen and Captain Scott.

During the International Geophysical Year (IGY), Antarctica was crossed from sea to sea by the team of explorers headed by Vivian Fuchs with the co-operation of Edmund Hillary. Their work included the investigation of the polar ice-cap; the rocks and off-shore waters of Antarctica; its weather in relation to the world's climate; its skies, including such phenomena as the Southern Lights; and its wild life. So satisfactory was such work that the Antarctic treaty of 1959 sought to place it on a permanent basis.

The IGY was marked, too, by the launching by Russia and then the United States, of the first artificial satellites. The information these transmitted threw light on conditions in the upper air; on the Earth's gravitation, magnetism and electricity; on the Sun's radiation and cosmic rays; and on the grains of extra-terrestrial dust known as micro-meteors.

The pioneer satellites heralded the exploration of conditions beyond the Earth's atmosphere by unmanned and manned space capsules. These, transmitting much valuable information back to Earth, have soared around the Moon and approached Mars and Venus.

In July 1969, two American astronauts landed on the Moon, erected apparatus to record conditions on its surface and collected specimens of its rocks. Now being intensively studied, these should throw new light on the nature of the Earth and the development of the Universe.

In July and November 1969 two American astronauts landed on the Moon, collected rock specimens and set up scientific apparatus.

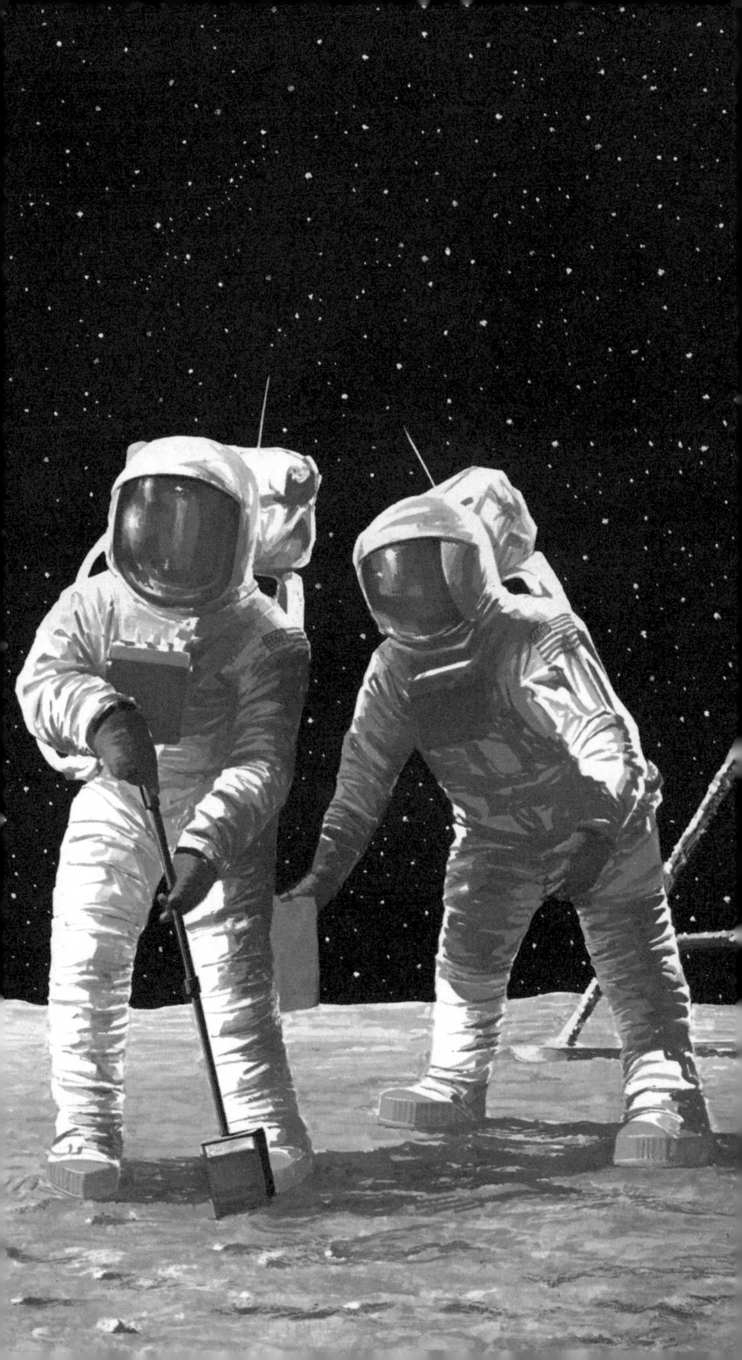

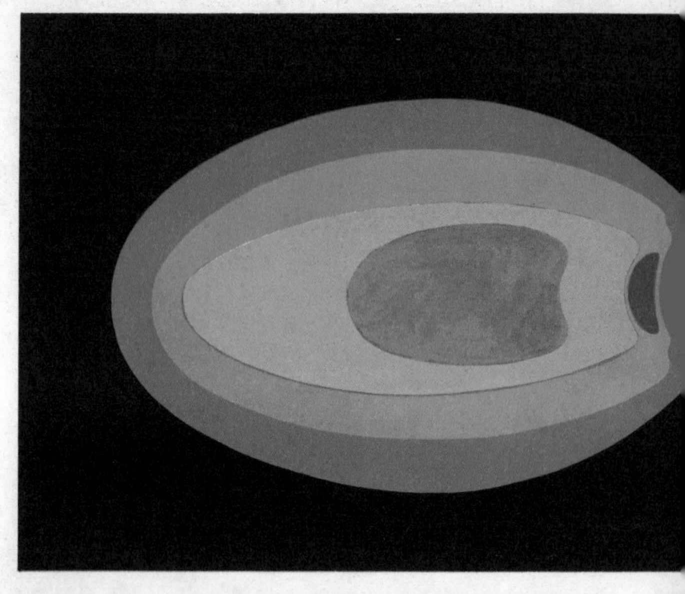

The Van Allen belts, part of the Earth's geomagnetic field

The Earth in space

Information received from the artificial satellites shows that the Earth is surrounded by a complicated magnetic field, and in 1958 it revealed the existence of the Van Allen belts, zones of high-energy particles extending thousands of miles into space. 'Solar winds', streams of electrified particles hurled outwards from the sun, compress this field on one side of the Earth to within 40,000 miles of its surface, while on the other it forms a 'tail' about 120,000 miles long pointing away from the Sun. The interaction of these particles produces the aurorae, but what other effects it may have is uncertain; it might constitute a serious hindrance to space travel.

The development of radio astronomy has analysed the radio waves that the Earth receives from the Sun and planets and from beyond the Solar System. Jupiter emits powerful radio waves, and those coming from within the Milky Way confirm the resemblance of its structure to that of the spiral nebulae. Some of these, arriving from beyond the Milky

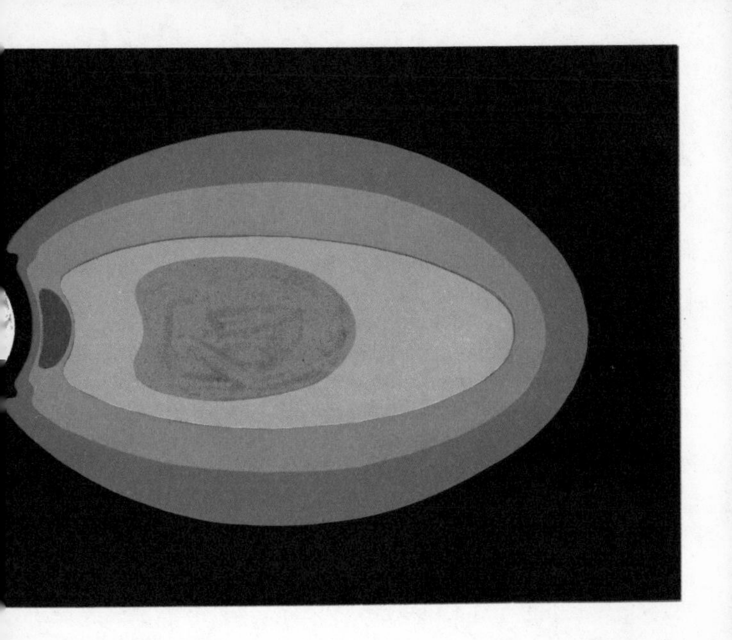

Way have been correlated with visible objects found, in 1963, to be very far distant. Such objects must be extremely bright to be visible at such a distance and are called *quasars* (quasi-stellar objects) but their exact nature is unknown.

The theory that the Earth was ripped from the Sun by the approach of another star is no longer accepted. The whole Solar System is now thought to have developed from a cloud of dust and gas similar to the clouds known to exist within the Milky Way. This cloud slowly condensed; its centre part, rotating and becoming intensely hot, formed the Sun, and eddies within it produced the planets and satellites – including the Earth.

Similar dust clouds may have produced the double and multiple star systems within the Galaxy, and some of the systems thus formed may include planets capable of supporting life. No longer, therefore, need we assume that in all the Universe our own Earth may be the only place where life, as we know it, is able to exist.

This our world

Recent advances have modified some geological theories and confirmed others. We now believe not, as had long been thought, that the Earth has been cooling down from a state of intense heat but that it has been getting warmer from a state of intense cold.

We are satisfied that, apart from a few doubtful exceptions, the objects once called 'figured stones' and dismissed as mere 'freaks of nature', are really what they seem to be, the fossilized remains of long-perished animals and plants.

We agree with Werner that some rocks were formed as a sediment on the sea floor; with Hutton that others have risen in a molten state from within the Earth; and with Lyell that the former changes of the Earth's surface can be explained by reference to causes now in operation – though some causes were formerly more effective than they are now.

While most of us accept evolution as a fact, opinions still differ as to its cause.

No longer can we regard the Earth as a mere inert mass of rock hurtling round the Sun. We now realize that its very substance is in incessant motion, from the downward creep of soil on hillside slopes to the swirl of molten material at the Earth's core. The Earth is active and ever-changing; we might even call it 'alive' in the sense that we speak of a 'live wire', for the magnetic and other forces that it generates interact with the forces that reach it from outer space.

There are still many problems to be solved; Earth-lore, of which geology is a part, may be only in its infancy.

Finally, we now interpret Noah's Flood not as a world-wide but as a local inundation and Genesis I as a statement not of fact but of faith, the faith that 'In the beginning God created the heavens and the earth.' And the modern theory that both the heavens and the Earth developed from an inchoate dust cloud might well be expressed in the words:

'And the earth was without form and void; and darkness was upon the face of the deep.'

In August 1957 the huge radio-telescope at Jodrell Bank became operational. A reflector, 250ft in diameter, enables more accurate studies of the heavens to be made.

Books to Read

Works on the history of geology

The Birth and Development of the Geological Sciences by Frank Dawson Adams. Constable, London, 1938, republished 1954. A very full treatment, arranged under subjects. Copiously illustrated.

A Century of Science in America by E. A. Dana et al. Yale University Press, Newhaven; Cambridge University Press, 1918.

The Earth in Decay: A History of British Geomorphology 1578–1878 by G. L. Davies. Macdonald Technical and Scientific Books, London, 1969. A full and very illuminating treatment of the various theories framed to explain the Earth's surface features. A few illustrations.

The Earth is Alive by François Derrey translated by Gregor Roy. Arlington Books, London (Editions Planete, Paris). A discussion of many fascinating theories regarding the Earth and its relation to the Universe. Unillustrated.

The Earth We Live On: the Story of Geological Discovery by Ruth Moore. Jonathan Cape, London, 1957. More popular in tone, but more up-to-date than some of the other works. Illustrated.

Fifty Years Retrospect by the Royal Society of Canada. Anniversary Volume, 1882–1952, The Society, 1952. Includes five papers on various aspects of geology.

The Founders of Geology by Sir Archibald Geikie. Macmillan, London, 1897; revised and enlarged 1905. Biographical; deals chiefly with the 'Heroic Age of Geology' from the middle of the eighteenth to the early nineteenth century. Unillustrated.

Genesis and Geology: A study in the Relations of Scientific Thought, Natural Theology and Social Opinion in Great Britain, 1790–1850 by Charles Coulston Gillespie. Harper and Brothers, New York, 1951. Not an attempt to 'reconcile' the two but an exhaustive account of the efforts made to do so. Unillustrated.

The Geological Survey of Great Britain by E. B. Bailey. Thomas Murby, London, 1952.

History of Geology by H. B. Woodward. Watts, London, 1911. A brief treatment of the subject. Portraits.

Science in its Context: A Symposium with special reference to sixth form studies by John Brierley. Heinemann, London, 1964.

INDEX

Page numbers in bold type refer to illustrations

SOME OTHER TITLES IN THIS SERIES

- Arts
- Domestic Animals and Pets
- Domestic Science
- Gardening
- General Information
- History and Mythology
- Natural History
- Popular Science

Arts
Antique Furniture/Architecture/Clocks and Watches/Glass for Collectors/Jewellery/Musical Instruments/Porcelain/Pottery/Victoriana

Domestic Animals and Pets
Budgerigars/Cats/Dog Care/Dogs/Horses and Ponies/Pet Birds/Pets for Children/Tropical Freshwater Aquaria/Tropical Marine Aquaria

Domestic Science
Flower Arranging

Gardening
Chrysanthemums/Garden Flowers/Garden Shrubs/House Plants/Plants for Small Gardens/Roses

General Information
Aircraft/Arms and Armour/Coins and Medals/Flags/Fortune Telling/Freshwater Fishing/Guns/Military Uniforms/Motor Boats and Boating/National Costumes of the world/Orders and Decorations/Rockets and Missiles/Sailing/Sailing Ships and Sailing Craft/Sea Fishing/Trains/Veteran and Vintage Cars/Warships

History and Mythology
Age of Shakespeare/Archaeology/Discovery of: Africa/The American West/Australia/Japan/North America/South America/Great Land Battles/Great Naval Battles/Myths and Legends of: Africa/Ancient Egypt/Ancient Greece/Ancient Rome/India/The South Seas/Witchcraft and Black Magic

Natural History
The Animal Kingdom/Animals of Australia and New Zealand/Animals of Southern Asia/Bird Behaviour/Birds of Prey/Butterflies/Evolution of Life/Fishes of the world/Fossil Man/A Guide to the Seashore/Life in the Sea/Mammals of the world/Monkeys and Apes/Natural History Collecting/The Plant Kingdom/Prehistoric Animals/Seabirds/Seashells/Snakes of the world/Trees of the world/Tropical Birds/Wild Cats

Popular Science
Astronomy/Atomic Energy/Chemistry/Computers at Work/The Earth/Electricity/Electronics/Exploring the Planets/Heredity
The Human Body/Mathematics/Microscopes and Microscopic Life/Physics/Undersea Exploration/The Weather Guide